PAT EASTMAN

Up in the Air

*An aviator's wife's story of early days
of commercial aviation from 1924 to 1938*

*Best wishes,
Mary M. Worthylake*

by Mary M. Worthylake

Mary M. Worthylake, Publisher
1881 Country Club Road
Woodburn, Oregon 97071

Dedicated To:

...My children: Margaret Louise (Margie Lou), who died too young.
Frank (once called Teddy), who also has a pilot's license.
Mary Jo, my dear younger daughter.

...To all the pilot's wives I have known over the years.

...And to Joe—thanks for the memories.

"You don't seem to mind it! How long will you be away? she asked.

A week or ten days, he couldn't say. "Mind it?" Why should he? All those cities, plains, and mountains... In freedom he was going out to conquer them...

She thought of all a man must lay aside to conquer. "So you don't like your home?" "I do like my home."

But his wife knew that he was already on his way and even now his sturdy shoulders were pressing up against the sky...

He shut the door behind him and...took the first step toward his conquests.

She remained, sadly looking at these flowers and books, little friendly things which meant for him no more than the bottom of the sea.

From *Night Flight,* by Antoine de Saint-Exupery.
N.Y.: Reynal and Hitchcock, Inc. 1932

Table of Contents

CHAPTER ONE

My Introduction to a Young Aviator - 1924

Grandpa and I were walking to church on a sunny March day in 1924. The sky was a bright blue and Mt. San Jacinto's snowy peak gleamed white above the green hills. The tang of eucalyptus leaves filled the air.

Suddenly San Jacinto's Sunday morning quiet was shattered by the buzzing of an airplane which zoomed into view above the bungalows and the ragged trees.

"Must be that Barrows kid come home for a visit," Grandpa said, shading his eyes to peer upward, his gray beard wagging in disapproval. "Just look at that crazy fool, and on Sunday, too. He'll be killing himself one of these days. His parents are real nice folks, too."

I had met Mr. and Mrs. Barrows a few days before, and they *were* real nice folks. Mr. Barrows, a conductor on the Santa Fe local, was interested to learn that I had taught school two years on the southern Oregon coast. We agreed on the beauty of the Pacific Northwest. Mr. Barrows said he would like to get his deer in the fall without crawling through sun-baked, rattlesnake infested brush.

That afternoon from Grandpa's windows I watched the stunting airplane, hearing the clatter of the old OX5 motor as the pilot carried passengers over town, with or without stunts as requested. He even looped the loop around the flagpole in the village center for an extra consideration. In those days there weren't any laws regulating airplanes or air traffic. There wasn't any air traffic.

About sunset a shadow passed silently over the house and the plane slipped down into a cow pasture across the road for a deadstick landing. The pilot climbed out of the open cockpit, pulled off his helmet to reveal flaming red hair, and jerked up the motor cowling to work on the engine. I saw that he was tall and slim, dressed in a brown sweater, breeches and boots.

That evening Grandpa and I were invited to the Barrows home and I met Joe. He was only twenty but had been flying four years, soloing in 1920 at the age of sixteen at the old Mercury Field in Los Angeles. He tried to enlist in the Army Air Corps at March Field but his parents felt that sixteen was too young for Army life and instead had financed his aviation course. After flying around Los

1

Angeles for two years he went home to San Jacinto and finished high school.

He had been barnstorming around San Diego and now, at home, had agreed to instruct a few students. One of these was Milo Campbell, who later flew on one of the transcontinental air lines.

Marjorie, Joe's sister, and her husband were visiting from Los Angeles and the trio furnished music. Joe played the piano, his sister the violin, and her husband sang. "Beautiful Ohio", "Mexicali Rose", "Missouri Waltz" were popular airs at the time. Later Joe took us home in his father's Dodge touring car.

"Would you like to take an airplane ride some day?" he asked me.

Until that moment I had never desired to leave the ground but suddenly flying was the one thing I had always wanted to do.

Two days later I had my first flight in the JN4D—"Jenny" to World War I pilots. I pulled a leather helmet over the puffs and coils of my long hair, which I wore fluffed out in "cootie garages" over my ears. Goggles covered part of my face. Hobbled by a long, tight skirt, I climbed awkwardly into the front cockpit. Long skirts and long hair were just going out of style. I had wanted to bob my hair but my Oregon county school superintendent said he wouldn't have a bobbed-haired teacher in his county. A teacher couldn't possibly maintain either dignity or discipline with short hair!

The plane bumped over the uneven stubble of the field and wavered into the air over a fence, just cleared a row of eucalyptus trees, and labored up to the dizzy height of seven hundred feet. Below me I saw Grandpa feeding his chickens, unaware of my daring flight. In years to come the old man, who was born in Vermont and had homesteaded in Dakota Territory and in Colorado, never did quite realize the extent or significance of aviation.

"Tain't in reason for aery-o-planes to fly back and forth across oceans," he said at age ninety-two, shaking his head in actual disbelief that Joe had flown across the Pacific and back again. That was several years in the future.

I paid for my flight over the orange groves with a piece of homemade pie, for I had heard about the way to a man's heart, and within the next two weeks I had two more flights. On the third I sat in the rear cockpit and turned gadgets as Joe yelled,

"Switch off and choke."

Then I flicked a switch at the shout of "contact" and the propellor spun, Joe leaping quickly to safety from the whirling blades. After we were in the air I had my first lesson in dual flying, guiding the plane by myself while Joe held his hands in the air to show that I was actually in control. I didn't solo until eight years

2

later, and Joe wasn't my instructor then.

Between flights we hiked into the hills, cooked suppers over campfires, and generally neglected my grandfather and Joe's small class of students. Then I received a letter from Oregon, enclosing a contract, asking me to teach a term of summer school in a reorganized district near my uncle's ranch on the Chetco River, the school to start the first of May.

Grandpa decided to go north with me as he was still a little lost after my grandmother's death, which had brought me to San Jacinto. Just a month after I met the redheaded aviator, I was on the train going back to Oregon—and I was engaged. Joe would solo all of his students before starting north. Then he planned to assemble a surplus Army plane he had purchased, another Jenny powered with an Hispano-Suisa motor. We planned to be married in June and to honeymoon on the Oregon coast while I finished my summer term of school. That's what we planned! But the best laid plans of mice and men—

My school was four miles up the Chetco River from Brookings, which was then a thriving sawmill town. The coast highway had not yet been built and Curry County was quite isolated. In winter it took four hours by Model T to drive to Gold Beach, the county seat, due to the muddy, deep-rutted roads. The people along the Chetco River had never seen an airplane, at least not around there, and when they heard that I was expecting one to land nearby I was the center of attraction.

"Better get him to take out lots of insurance," the chairman of my school board advised. "An aviator's wife is sure to be a young widow."

At that time no commercial aviator could get insurance in any amount. The next year or so Joe got a policy for $690, at a stiff premium. He was told he might double it sometime in the future, if he wasn't killed in the meantime.

"Of course you'll get him to change his occupation," my friends said. "Surely you don't want a husband who *flies*!" This in the same tone of voice as used in speaking of a man who drank, or bet his salary on the horses, or held up banks. "Flying might be all right for some young sport, but it ain't the thing for a family man. You'll get him to stop it, won't you?"

When I said I intended to fly with him they shook their heads sadly, in their imaginations already pulling my mangled corpse from a flaming mass of wreckage.

Joe asked me to find a landing field for him, seemingly impossible in that timbered country. I didn't know then that ocean beaches or river bars were the best landing sites. Young fliers today can't visualize a time when there were no commercial fields,

3

no emergency landing field at all staked out with runways, border lights, or even wind socks.

Joe's letters were logs of difficulties as he tried to assemble a plane that was in an advanced state of decay. No parts were available locally and he made frequent trips to Los Angeles or San Diego hoping to find some war surplus materials. He described one flight from San Jacinto to San Diego:

"May 22. San Diego. Arrived about noon today after a thrilling trip. We had two forced landings coming down and were flying in the fog out of sight of the ground a good part of the way. We had our forced landings in some rough and rugged places but got away with them. Parts for the Hisso motor are hard to find.

"I was propositioned by some Mexicans who wanted me to fly for them way down in southern Mexico where there never have any planes. I turned them down.

"We are carrying passengers for $2.50 a ride now and I expect to do better than at $5.00. More can afford to ride and I've got to do something to raise some cash."

On May 28th he wrote:

"I've had quite a time fixing the plane to carry enough gas and oil for the longest flights. Then I'll have to carry a spare wheel, tires, some tools, spare parts, etc., so I'll surely be loaded down. I'll leave here so I can cross the Mojave Desert early. Then I'll eat breakfast in Fresno, dinner at Redding, and supper with you—I hope."

He didn't make it then, but at last, one Saturday noon at the end of June the farmer's community line telephone rang my uncle's particular call. I got the following telegram which was phoned up from Brookings:

"Plan to leave four a.m. Saturday. May not make trip in one day but if everything goes right shall be there Saturday evening. Do not worry if I am delayed as I may need repairs in Sacramento."

I heard receivers click along the party line so I knew all the neighbors were aware that the schoolma'am's beau was on his way. Lunch was forgotten. I dived into a clean middy blouse, knotted a red tie around the collar, and hurried out to my Model T. I kept it parked on a hill in Uncle Frank's apple orchard so that on school mornings I could start easily by giving it a shove down grade—the starter never did work. With hand throttle open, I negotiated the winding road down the river.

I waited in Harbor until sundown but no airplane arrived. Mark and Bertha Wood, owners of the Harbor general store, asked me to spend the night. The next day we picnicked on the beach and kept watch for a plane. That day, and on the following ones, I had my first taste of what it meant to be an aviator's wife, listening for the

4

sound of an airplane motor, watching weather conditions, preparing meals which went uneaten, waiting— waiting—

When it was too dark to see I drove back up the Chetco.

The next morning, just as I was leaving for school, the phone rang.

"Mary, he's here!" Bertha Wood's voice was breathless with excitement. "He's circling around right now looking for a place to land. Come down right away."

School and duty were forgotten as I drove as fast as the Model T could make the curves. At the Harbor store all the village's forty-five inhabitants were out in the road, rubbing their necks after staring skyward. They had just seen the first airplane to fly over that section of the Oregon coast.

"I guess he couldn't land here," Mark Wood said as I stopped with the motor running. "He went on south. You'll probably find him in the first big field you come to."

So on down the coast I went. At each ranch people were standing in the road and everyone told me that the plane has just gone out of sight to the south. At the California line I had to stop to run the car tires through sheep dip. At the time there was a hoof and mouth disease scare. I questioned the quarantine officer and he looked as if he thought I was crazy. (Uncle Frank would have seconded that!)

At Smith River I stopped and phoned to Crescent City, learning that the plane had landed there and that the pilot, Vernon Brookwalter from Portland, had come to carry passengers over the Fourth of July. Years later when I met Vernon Brookwalter up in Skagway, Alaska, I told him how I had nearly lost my job chasing his plane down the Oregon coast that morning.

Disappointed and worried, I started back up the Chetco, tardily remembering that I was supposed to be teaching school. My active imagination pictured all manner of dire things which might have happened to Joe. A day or so later I received a telegram saying he had started but had broken a propellor and had to have a new one made. The next wire said he had radiator trouble over the Mojave desert and had to turn back. A letter of explanation read in part:

"Sunday morning I took off at 4:30 a.m. In 40 minutes I was over the Cajon Pass and coming out over the desert. The motor was getting hot and the radiator had been boiling for quite a while. There are a hundred miles of desert to cross at this point so I decided to go back as far as San Bernardino and fix the radiator. I started back and it's a good thing I did because I kept losing altitude and expected the motor to quit altogether or catch on fire at any time, but it didn't. I sure had an exciting ride back over the mountains for 30 miles. I passed as close as 30 feet to the trees and

5

mountain sides with no landing places in sight. I reached San Bernardino all right and landed safely beside the cemetery.

"Worked on the radiator and filled it and took off but the thermometer came up again so I headed for home but had to land between Beaumont and Redlands along the railroad and put in more water. I took off again and barely made it over the San Jacinto ridge and into my field. I've got to go to work for a few days as I've spent all the money I had. I've put over $150 on the plane in the last two weeks."

All summer I listened for the sound of an airplane motor. In the evenings I sat on an old log jutting out over the Chetco River at the ford, hoping a silver-winged airplane would glide down to land on the river bar's gravel. My school was pleasant and the children were a joy, but my mind was not undividedly in the classroom with my nine little boys and girls.

Finally on August 15th I received a letter postmarked from Chico, up in the Sacramento Valley, saying he had left home at 5 a.m. and reached Stockton by 12:30. He stayed at Sacramento until the evening cooled and then reached Chico, where he had to repair a valve. Here he waited for six weeks, repairing his engine and ordering parts. During this time he worked in a garage to earn his daily bread.

"Even if my plane were repaired there is no business here carrying passengers. People aren't sold on aviation. There is a pilot here now with a plane and he is almost starving."

The last week in September he wired that he would be on his way to Ashland. We had arranged to be married at my father's home there and I asked the school board to give me two days off. I took the stage from Crescent City across to Grants Pass—an all-day trip winding around the mountain tops on a narrow road.

My father's big, old-fashioned house sat high on a hill overlooking the town. A porch extended across the front and around one side and was almost buried beneath a huge English ivy vine. The downstairs rooms had ceilings at least twelve feet high and a carved wooden staircase went up from a reception hall. There were three fireplaces in the house, but no furnace. The ornately carved mantel on one fireplace bore an inscription, "East or West, Hame's the Best." When we moved into the house we children thought "Hame" was the man who had built the fireplace and that this was his advertising slogan. We had moved to Ashland in 1918 from the bare prairies of eastern Colorado and we were sure this house was one of the most luxurious homes in the world. We had never had plumbing before, and this house had two toilets. There were even two stairways, and a speaking tube from the upstairs hall to the kitchen—probably to summon a servant back in the 1870's when servants were still to be had. In this house my youngest sister, Dorothy, was born and here my mother had died.

Joe had arrived in Ashland before I did and flew down to Grants Pass to pick me up, learning that I had to wait there to change buses. But I had spent my time in a beauty parlor, getting a marcel for my newly bobbed hair and under the drier I hadn't heard the airplane fly over.

Much later Joe admitted that he had landed without any money, using his last dollar to pay for the marriage license. With no money to give to the minister, or to buy gasoline, he went downtown to wire to his friends at the Chico garage for help. Fearing the money might not come in time, or that they could not send any, he pawned his revolver for ten dollars. For years he joked that he was so broke he had to 'hock' his gun to pay the preacher.

A local dressmaker in Brookings had made my dress of material ordered from Sears Roebuck. The result was not a success. The material was a heavy Canton crepe in a bilious greenish-blue shade. The shape was that of a gunny sack with holes for the head and arms—a sheath style. For 98¢ in the catalogue I had also bought a bunch of fancy silver flowers which the advertisement said could be worn either on the shoulder or on the belt. I tacked them nattily on the front of the dropped-waistline belt over my stomach.

My married sister, Myrtle, arrived with her husband and small son. My three little sisters were excited about having a wedding right in their own house, and my high-school age brothers decided the ocasion warranted a shave so they held up the bathroom. The only guests were the minister and his wife and the family doctor and his wife. I had been away from Ashland four years going to college and teaching and my own friends had all married and moved away.

The minister's wife played a wedding march and I came down the front stairs into the reception room. It was separated from the living room by a bead curtain made of little rolls of newspaper shellacked and strung with colored glass beads. Joe and I stood in the doorway while the minister pronounced the solemn words. I began to cry; after all, I had known Joe only a month down in Southern California. Then my brother Frank caught my eye and winked at me and back of the wink was all the companionship we had shared over the years, the memory of horseback trips we had taken together, of our summers at the family ranch in the Dead Indian valley.

I heard Joe repeating solemnly, "With all my worldly goods I thee endow," and my tears dried as I couldn't help grinning. He didn't have any worldly goods except the Hisso-Jenny which was mortgaged from the propellor to the rudder.

While Myrtle and my stepmother prepared cake and ice cream the minister's wife played and sang hymns. Her first selection was ''Rescue the Perishing.'' I have always thought that song singularly appropriate for wedding music.

The next morning Frank was able to round up a few high school friends for airplane rides, at reduced rates, and Joe had money to buy some gasoline.

About two in the afternoon we took for what we expected to be a short two hour flight across the Coast Range Mountains to Crescent City.

CHAPTER TWO

Honeymoon in the Air

Honeymoons in the air were not routine in September of 1924, and mine certainly wasn't. In fact, it earned publicity in the majority of West Coast newspapers.

Joe had landed in a field across Bear Creek from Ashland. Now, the day after our wedding, I first saw the plane which he had laboriously assembled from World War I spare parts and which had taken him all the summer to fly from San Jacinto, California up to Ashland, Oregon.

The wings were silver-colored, the veneer-wood fuselage was a sage green, and my first impression was that it must be the most beautiful plane in the world. However, my knowledge of airplanes was not very extensive.

The Hisso-Jenny had been a jinxed airplane from the start, forcing Joe to turn back over the Mojave Valley when it developed radiator trouble, and blowing a valve over Chico. Now we hoped troubles were behind us.

It was County Fair time in Crescent City, California, and toward this fair we were heading. Joe hoped to carry enough passengers at $2.50 a ride, or at $5.00 a ride with stunts, to put some cash in his empty wallet.

Nattily dressed for the flight, I wore knee-length knickers, a white middy blouse, gray silk stockings, and pumps. I took off my new gray felt hat for which I had paid $5.98 at a Crescent City milliner's and adjusted my new helmet over my marcelled bob. Then I performed the "switch-off-and-choke" routine. As Joe called "contact" and prepared to spin the prop, we heard a buzzing in the sky. Headlines had featured the Army's round-the-world flight. Now these illustrious airplanes were crossing overhead, bound that day for Eugene. Our Jenny leaped into the air after them, as a barnyard gander which heard the call from a band of wild geese.

Before we were up fifteen minutes I was spattered with hot water, and soon steam was streaming back from the radiator. It was boiling again, as it had boiled all the way up from Southern California. Joe landed in a cow pasture near Central Point and we went to a creek to fill two canteens with water. The canteens were

9

part of the emergency equipment. Several cars raced up and stopped beside the road.

"Are you one of the round-the-world fliers?" came the eager questions.

"No!" Joe denied the claim but looked important to be considered, with the old Jenny, in that exalted class.

After the radiator cooled we took off, but less than five miles farther, beyond the Gold Hill cement plant, we were forced down again. This time Joe decided to remove the radiator and clean it.

Two boys were hired to watch the Jenny overnight to protect it from a bull which shared the pasture with us. If he decided to charge it his horns could easily puncture the fabric-covered wings.

That afternoon and all day Sunday Joe and a local mechanic worked on the radiator while I answered questions of interested on-lookers. My quiet, schoolma'am life hadn't prepared me to be part of a traveling circus. Actually, in 1924 aviation was in the same category as pilots earned a living by stunt flying, by carrying passengers on short flights, or by "flying circus" acts.

"You couldn't hire me to go up in one of them things," was the usual comment. "I want to keep one foot on the ground."

Monday morning we took off while it was cool, in case the motor still overheated. I was due at my school, up the Chetco River from Brookings, at nine o'clock.

Joe noticed after we got into the air that the gas gauge was no longer working.

There was a heavy head wind and black clouds lay along the Coast Range summit. As we approached we saw a solid mass of billowing fog which stretched to the western horizon. Beneath this mass were hills and giant redwoods, and Joe didn't dare go down through into strange terrain.

We hadn't gas enough left to get back to the Illinois River Valley. Joe circled, looking for a place to land. A tiny ranch in the bottom of the canyon was a possibility and he swooped down. Tall fir trees bordered the small field, a field too small for safety, so he climbed back up out of the canyon.

The motor coughed on the last gas in the tank.

Joe unfastened his safety belt, stood up in the rear cockpit and leaned over to kiss me goodbye. I figured he was going to crash the plane so we would be killed instantly, instead of suffering. We were going to die together, and only three days after our marriage!

"Brace your feet and cover your head!" he shouted.

I was so busy watching I couldn't cover my face.

Nearer came the side of the mountain, until I could distinguish each separate boulder, each scrub pine tree.

We came in over the canyon a thousand feet below. Above us

rose the side of the mountain. As I braced for the crash Joe nosed the plane up and set it down gently in a little pocket he had seen on the steep slope.

Two tires exploded, cut by the rocks. We plowed forward a few feet and stopped, not twenty yards from the canyon's edge. A dead pine was toppled in our path; a boulder was moved.

Joe jumped out to assess the damage and found none except to the tires and to a wing's fabric where a small pine tree thrust up through a jagged tear. The prop still rotated. There sat the plane among the rocks.

I unfastened my safety belt and scrambled out. I wasn't shaking and hadn't been frightened; things had happened too fast.

Nothing was to be gained by staying with the plane so Joe lifted out my small bag and our sweaters. From the tool box he took a jar of vegetable boullion his sister had given him, jokingly, for emergency rations. This was our food supply.

We started walking west. Joe kept looking back at the plane which was his sole support, and yet which had caused him unlimited trouble all summer and which had now let him down on his honeymoon.

While he was circling over the fog Joe had seen a road which I assumed was the main highway from Grants Pass to Crescent City, so we walked in that direction. It was about time for the daily stage, or we might hail a car headed for the coast.

"It would be lots more of an adventure if we miss the stage and have to camp out," Joe commented.

After about three miles of scrambling over rocks we reached the road, and found it only an untraveled trail. The only tracks in it were deer hoofprints. I guessed it was the old wagon road to the early-day Monumental Mines, and learned later that this was correct. The Jenny sat almost exactly on the Oregon-California line.

Fall rains had not yet started and the brush was dry. All day we found no water and we had foolishly left the canteens in the plane in our desire to travel light. And during the whole day we saw no sign of human passage along the old road. This section of the Coast Range was then almost uninhabited.

About dusk we came to a spring of cold, delicious water. Rain clouds in the sky made us think about shelter for the night. Tacked to a tree was a crude sign lettered, "Happy Camp ½ mile" and we took the trail pointing down the valley. Happy Camp was only an abandoned cabin near a prospect hole, but another spring bubbled beside it. In the cabin was a rusty stove, a bench, and a pile of musty hay. Nothing more. We heated boullion in a tin pail we found and tried to sleep on the dusty hay. During the night it

11

began to rain and the air grew cold. Dawn came slowly, wet and disagreeable.

At daylight we drank more hot boullion, nourishing but not filling for a day of hiking. I left a note, wondering who might read it someday.

My light pumps were cut to pieces from the rocks and Joe's riding boots had made blisters on his heels. We were both limping badly as we stumbled along the old trail. With each passing hour we walked more and more slowly and paused longer to rest. The adventure was assuming serious proportions.

About noon we topped a ridge and looked down into a little green valley. At the far end was a cabin with smoke issuing from a chimney. Half an hour later we approached an old man who was splitting wood under a wide-spreading myrtle tree. He dropped his axe in the astonishment of seeing strangers. He was a prospector who had been working a little copper mine for twenty-six years. He had never seen an airplane but recalled hearing our motor above the fog the morning before.

"Where are we?" asked Joe.

"How far is it to the coast?" I asked.

"It's about nine miles down to Smith River," the miner replied.

Hospitably he heated up a kettle of beans and stirred up hotcakes from his sourdough jar. The hot food tasted good and we probably ate him out of a week's groceries.

I saw a telephone and found that it was connected with the forest service line. Ringing the lookout station at the top of Mt. Emily, I asked the ranger there to relay a message down to my aunt on the Chetco River to tell her where we were and to get word to my pupils that there would be school the next day.

Nine miles seemed comparatively short, now that we had a definite goal, but it was raining in earnest when we set out. Soon we were beneath the redwoods, and the walking was easier on the soft needle-covered ground.

Some hours later, drenched to the skin, we reached Rowdy Creek to find that the footbridge was washed out. Holding hands, we waded into the waist-deep water. The current nearly swept us off our feet, but we plunged across and hurried on, dripping and shivering. The whistle of donkey engines and the chugging of the logging train heralded our return to a peopled area.

Moments later we saw a friend washing clothes on her back porch. She laughed as she recognized me and began to sing, "here comes the bride." A more bedraggled bridal pair were never seen. Soon we were in dry clothes, with ours steaming beside the stove. When her logger-husband came home we ate again, and then were taken up the Chetco River to my Uncle Frank's ranch, where I was boarding.

While I taught school Joe and a ranger, George Bearse, made plans to go back to Packsaddle Mountain to salvage the airplane. They would go on horseback, carrying two five-gallon cans of gasoline on a pack horse. Joe felt that it was feasible to clear a runway and fly the Jenny out. The runway would be short, but by taking off downhill, when he reached the canyon's edge his speed would catapault the plane into the air a thousand feet above the canyon floor. So he hoped—

The fourth day their food gave out so they hastily finished grubbing out a runway and Joe decided to try a take-off. Gas was poured into the tank, the plane's tail pulled back into the brush as far as possible, and the motor revved up. George took a snapshot for me, just in case.

The plane was gathering flying speed when a tire caught on a snag and blew out. The Jenny wobbled into the air and was a few feet high when it hit the pine trees, nosed over, and splintered the propellor.

Again, little damage was done. There were some rips in the wing fabric, a broken prop, another punctured tire. But Joe decided not to try again. Hungry and discouraged, the men rode back.

My school term finished the next week and we moved to Crescent City, renting a two-room apartment over a grocery store. A young Indian living nearby owned an old Jenny but did not know how to fly. In exchange for lessons Joe arranged to fly the Jenny until he could salvage our plane. We hired a Smith River rancher to drive up with horses and wagon to bring out the wreckage.

"We'll see you at Pine Flat next Wednesday, rain or shine?"

"Yes, rain or shine," agreed the rancher.

Monday we drove my Ford to the road's end at Winchuck Ranger Station, then hiked about seven miles to Packsaddle Mountain where George Bearse was spending the winter trapping. Snow and high winds held us there over a day but Wednesday we headed for Pine Flat on George's horses. We were dressed in his foul-weather gear—tin pants, slickers and rubber boots, and carried chunks of dried venison for rations.

On the ridge gale-force winds and stinging snow caused the horses to rear and plunge. The trail was slippery with ice and I doubted whether a team and wagon could possibly cross that rock-strewn ridge. That day a ship was wrecked in Crescent City harbor and the surf ran higher than in forty years.

When we reached the plane we tied the horses in the shelter of bushes and began loosening bolts which fastened the wings. The wind seized the first loosened wing surface, hurled it from our

13

hands and smashed it against a tree. Finally we had the four surfaces laid flat and anchored with rocks. We wound up the wires, tied the struts together, took out the landing gear bolts, and were ready to start back to Packsaddle when we saw the teamster coming through the snow.

He brought a tent which he lashed to the side of the wagon and we spent the night with him sleeping on hay. Twice the tent blew down over us. There was no dry wood for a fire so we divided our jerky and his pie for our supper.

Breakfastless and chilled to the bone, we worked in gale winds loading that fuselage into the wagon. It was a superhuman task without tackle or pulleys but at last we slid it forward into the wagon bed with the heavy motor in front under the seat. There was no use attempting to move the wings as their surfaces would catch the wind and overturn the wagon, so they were left for another trip.

It was nearly dark when we reached the old Monumental Mine road. We watched the wagon disappear in the falling snow. Later we learned that Ed had left the wagon and rode in the dark to the cabin of the copper miner who had fed us back in September. Next day he chopped trees from the road and built a section to detour around a fallen redwood. Rowdy Creek was so high he swam the horses across, leaving the wagon, which didn't reach Crescent City for a month.

The storm held us another two days at Packsaddle, then we hiked back to the ranger station over a brush-clogged trail, the swollen river forcing us to climb along the hillside the last two miles until we reached a swinging bridge. At midnight, when we reached Crescent City, I felt that the honeymoon was definitely over.

During the winter the rancher went back to Pine Flat for the wing surfaces and at last the whole unlucky airplane was in Crescent City. Joe never reassembled it, but sold it to an aviator in Eureka. I believe it crashed on its first test flight.

CHAPTER THREE

Barnstorming 1924-1926

Our two housekeeping rooms over the grocery store were at the southern end of Crescent City at the junction of roads south to Eureka and east to Grants Pass. The owner had a gas pump at the intersection, and behind the store were half a dozen one-room, dingy cabins which he called an auto court.

The store owner wanted to sell and made us a good offer. We realized we had to have something more than a precarious airplane-ride business to keep us eating. Joe said he could take care of the cabins in what tourist business we got, and I could tend the grocery store and the gas pump. The grocery stock inventoried at $384. I had a little money left from my $100 a month teacher's checks and we borrowed the remainder on my Ford. We signed papers and found ourselves in possession of a store and auto camp, obligated for payments of $60 a month.

There were two rooms downstairs behind the store and we moved into them. They were also dreary, with gray building paper on the walls. But the wood stove had a good oven and water coils so that we had both hot and cold running water at the sink. No bathroom. No other plumbing except the toilet and shower off the porch for the use of the campground people.

Storekeeping duties were not arduous, daily receipts seldom more than three dollars. When the rains started the last tourists disappeared and sales dropped to under a dollar a day—perhaps a loaf of bread, a can of pork and beans, a candy bar, and a can of tobacco. We had a roof over our heads and staple groceries to keep us from starvation. That was about all.

Joe went to work at once wiping the sand from the innards of the Jenny which was hangared down near the beach. But it developed chronic motor trouble and we had no money to repair it, nor did its owner. Joe seemed to be out of aviation for good.

However, an elderly townsman had taken an interest and decided there might be money in taxi and charter work. He offered Joe a partnership and said he would put up cash for a satisfactory plane. Accordingly, just before Christmas Joe left by bus for Los Angeles.

Kenneth Montee of Clover Field, Santa Monica was building a four-passenger cabin plane for us. Cabin planes were new and we expected to make a lot of money with this modern craft. (Of course, the pilot still sat outside in an open cockpit). Possession was retained by our backer, but Joe was to fly and keep the plane in repair for half the profits, to be divided after expenses were paid. Nothing was put into writing. We were babes in the woods regarding business.

I was alone over the holidays and for six weeks after. There was no business. Mud was deep and no car could enter the campground or reach the gas pump without getting stuck. It rained incessantly and my spirits were as gray as the wallpaper or the dripping skies outside. However, Christmas mail brought presents—blankets, table linen, towels, a clock. I bought bright cretonne to curtain the windows and a closet Joe had built in the bedroom, so our living quarters grew more cheerful.

The campground had its own electric plant and it invariably ran out of gas during the evening. Then I took my flashlight to wade through mud and teeter over boards laid across the swamp behind the store. I couldn't crank the balky water pump and relied on help from one of the men batching in one of the ramshackle cabins.

One wild, stormy morning a cyclone twisted up out of the ocean and whirled through the campground, picking up two of the cabins and the airplane hangar housing Harrison's Jenny. Boards flew through the air and smashed into splintered sticks. The next day I watched another black, funnel-shaped cloud swirl through the town. It struck about two hundred feet behind the main street, taking the roof from the rear of Hobbs-Wall store and whirling boards in crazy confusion as it twisted through the lumber yard and on into the timber.

In March, when Joe wrote that the plane had been tested, I got a woman to tend store and went to Ashland to meet him. He flew up from Los Angeles in a little over ten hours, a record trip. It took us only an hour and seventeen minutes to fly across to Crescent City.

The town gave us a royal welcome. People turned out en masse to greet us and the city band played while we circled overhead. The Chamber of Commerce gave Joe a dinner and even hired a tractor to grade a field above the beach for an emergency landing runway at high tide. The weekly paper came out with headlines across the front page, "Passenger Plane Arrives."

After our lean winter business picked up. One Sunday Joe took in seventy dollars in passenger fees. Three passengers chartered the plane for our first cross-country flight to Willits. But Joe landed on a field there which was under water, taxied into a ditch, and flipped the plane over. No one was badly hurt but the prop was broken, the tips of three wings damaged, and tail surfaces torn.

Our partner had moved into the upstairs apartment so, feeling

End of a honeymoon by air, September, 1924

First home, Crescent City, California. 1924

Beside the cabin plane

Cabin plane on the beach at Crescent City. 1925

Pilot on the San Diego-Los Angeles Air line. 1926

Looking for Trouble the Modern Way

W. J. (Joe) Barrows of the Pacific Coast Air Service piloting his Whirlwind Waco plane on one of his calls to survey a forest fire in Northern California. The two observers carried as passengers sketch the fire area and help direct the fire fighting program. This photo was taken from another plane also flying in the forest patrol service.

Newspaper picture of forest patrol.

Ryan's field, San Diego, 1926

Joe Barrows in cockpit. Mapping the Colorado River in a Ryan monoplane, 1926

that I needed a vacation, I left him in charge and caught a ride to Eureka, taking the train from there to Willits. On a borrowed sewing machine I made covers for the wings and tail. We had to wait for a new propellor and when the plane was repaired we were penniless again so Joe carried passengers for a few days to earn money for our hotel bill and to pay for welding and carpenter work debts.

Over the Fourth of July he went to Covelo to fly at a rodeo but a plane had crashed there recently, killing two local men, and people were afraid to fly.

Summer fog was our perpetual enemy, seeming to delight in keeping the plane grounded. If Joe flew to Eureka to work over a weekend fog might keep him there for days, unable to fly back home up the coast.

We saw no bright future in mere passenger rides on Sunday. We needed something more, like charter flights or a scheduled airline. But how to begin with no money to buy spare parts or extra propellors? One couldn't take hunters and fishermen into inaccessible mountain valleys and leave them there indefinitely while waiting for parts from back east.

Toward the end of July I was helping Joe put a bank of cylinders on the plane motor when a man came up asking for "the aviator." He introduced himself as Mr. Verne Gorst, from Marshfield, and said he was contemplating starting an airline up and down the Pacific coast. Since we had the only airplane in the country he wanted us to fly over the route and help him decide whether it would be more feasible to schedule flights along the coast or down the inland valleys.

A young couple in the campground agreed to tend things while we took this tour of inspection. Joe's brother, Robert, had just arrived for a visit and was thrilled at the thought of a long airplane trip. Bob was about thirteen then.

In the morning we started but had gone only a few miles when fog forced us down. We landed north of Point George, on the beach, visited the lighthouse, gathered agates, and had a picnic lunch. The fog dissolved in late afternoon and at low tide we took off, flying over Smith River, the Winchuck and the Chetco, over the school I had taught, over my uncle's ranch, and on up the coast. Joe planned to land at Port Orford because he heard that a plane had once landed there.

Port Orford bay is beautiful but the summer beach was soft. We landed on a tiny strip of sand and groundlooped up into regular dunes. The shelf above high tide was very narrow and I wondered if we'd ever get off again. A crowd of small boys gathered immediately and Joe selected two who appeared trustworthy and

17

offered them a plane ride if they would watch the plane overnight. A man hesitantly offered us a ride to town.

"Don't suppose you'd care to ride in a Ford," he apologized.

"Yours looks in better shape than ours," Joe replied.

By his disappointed look I guessed he expected us to own a Cadillac at least.

Our hotel rooms were lighted by kerosene lamps. Bob, from southern California, had never been in a place without running water or electricity. When I went to call him in the morning I found that he had pushed the bureau in front of the door so he wouldn't be attacked and murdered during the night.

Of course, it was foggy in the morning and by the time it cleared the tide was too high for a take off from the tiny beach. Next morning low tide was later and the fog was partially dispelled. Joe took the two young plane-watchers up for their promised ride. Then he motioned us to hurry to the plane. Waves were already washing around the wheels and wet our feet as we climbed in. As the wave ebbed Joe raced down the beach. I felt another wave catch at the wheels but we got off.

This day we almost made Coos Bay, where Mr. Gorst was expecting us, before the fog came in. We landed on a nice wide beach, rolled the plane up against the cliff, and caught a stage to town. Joe left Bob to watch the plane, promising to come back soon to relieve him. But once in town he got interesting in talking aviation and Bob sat hungry and alone for hours.

We were driven to inspect the proposed airport. It lay between North Bend and Marshfield, in a pocket with hills on three sides and with ditches across it. On the fourth side were high tension wires, a highway, and the bay. I never saw a field with more hazards. But a drive around North Bend disclosed nothing better. In late afternoon Joe took blankets to Bob and left him with another boy who wanted to be a pilot and thought sleeping under an airplane would be an introduction. We got a room at the hotel in North Bend.

However, a three dollar room was too expensive for us so I found a small apartment, with a cot for Bob, which we could rent for a week.

Joe brought the plane over to the little field but he didn't dare carry more than one passenger at a time from there.

Today one may land at an airport, order the plane serviced, and forget about it until time to leave, knowing it will be safe from souvenir hunters or curious people who might stand on the fabric of a wing or turn the prop. Then Bob and I spent our afternoons chasing people away. They had never seen an airplane before and wanted to examine this one minutely.

One gay young blade, with an admiring girl on each arm, sauntered up and peered into the cockpit.

"I used to fly one of these in France," he announced. "It's a pursuit plane. That," pointing to the control stick, "is the gear shift."

We ordered posters printed announcing that Joe would fly from the beach on Sunday so a number of people were there and Bob and I went along to solicit trade. We also shooed people back when Joe wanted to land or take off, racing breathlessly up to someone who sauntered out directly into the path of the landing plane.

"Why should I get off? This is a public beach," one man said hotly.

"I'm sorry, but if the propellor hit you, you'd be killed."

"Huh. You must think you own the beach!" he grunted as he walked slowly back.

No one was killed or maimed, though Bob and I pictured fatalities as we watched dear old ladies looking for agates, or small boys racing up and down the sand.

Toward the end of the week Joe had surveyed all the surrounding area for available airport sites and, his work done, was ready to return home. He was convinced that a coast route—at that time—would not be as practicable as an inland route from Portland through Eugene and Medford, primarily because of summer fogs. Before we got back to Crescent City we had proved it beyond the shadow of a doubt.

Mr. Gorst told us of a good beach from which we could take off as Joe wouldn't risk a take off with three of us in the plane. He flew across and Mr. Gorst drove us eighteen miles over what must have been one of the worst mountain roads in existence then, the "Seven Devils Road." There was a stiff wind and the plane bounced as it landed on the beach. Bob and Mr. Gorst held the wings while I climbed in with our suitcase. I saw that Joe was worried but he had already caused Mr. Gorst enough trouble for safety's sake so he decided to take a chance.

We said goodbye and Bob climbed in. Mr. Gorst released the wing and the plane rose straight up like a helicopter. We were about 300 feet up when a cross current from the top of the cliff struck us. The plane dropped sideways and completed the first turn of a tailspin. Bob threw his arms around my neck as we saw the water rising rapidly toward us.

Just before we hit Joe managed to straighten the plane out. The wheels hit the breakers but rolled toward shore. The plane taxied up out of the water and Joe kept on taxiing until we were at the foot of the cliff. Then he cut the switch and jumped out. He kissed me and Bob kissed both of us in the excitement and relief of being saved from a watery grave.

Without further ado Joe tied up the wings to driftwood logs. Then he took out the suitcase with a finality which told us he was through flying for the day.

We wouldn't let Mr. Gorst take us back to town but let him drop us at a large dairy ranch where we were welcomed.

For three days the wind howled and the sand blew. Every morning the fog was thick. Every afternoon it receded a little but stood menacingly out at sea in a heavy cloud, ready to roll in should we attempt to take off.

The farm wife was a superb cook and we had delicious seafood to eat. One morning I helped her prepare a dishpan full of crab salad for dinner for us and for the hired men who helped milk. Another time we took our noon meal across to another beach where the men were sawing driftwood logs. Here we boiled crabs and steamed clams over a campfire and roasted mussels in the flames.

Joe, Bob and I wandered along the beaches, picking up agates, exploring old deserted cabins in little coves, and talking to prospectors who shoveled black sand into little sluice boxes. One old man was scooping wet sand into a crude flume through which water ran. He stopped to rest behind a windbreak screen of gunny sacks and talked to us.

"About how much do you average a day?" Bob asked inquisitively.

"About twenty five," the old man answered.

At twenty five dollars a day we considered taking up shoveling black sand to salvage gold. It would be more profitable than flying. But afterward, recalling the poverty of the camp and the ragged appearance of the miner's overalls, we decided he meant cents instead of dollars.

The third morning the wind died down. Our farm hosts would only accept six dollars for their wonderful hospitality. We hurried to the beach and took off. After three minutes in the air we saw that the fog would win another round, but rather than go back Joe decided to push on south.

In ten minutes we were over Bandon, on the banks of the Coquille River. A lighthouse stood on the north bank and the beach looked smooth there, so as the fog thickened we landed beside the lighthouse. Leaving Bob as usual we signaled Coast Guard men to row us across the river.

Five days fog held us at Bandon, where we stayed at a seamanlike hotel. We inspected the life guard station, went swimming, hunted agates, explored the river and the beautiful beaches, nosed through fishing boats and walked out on the jetty. Every minute the fog horn uttered its doleful screech, never stopping, never varying the timing.

Joe usually managed to take up a passenger or two a day, in the late afternoon, to keep us in money for food and lodging. The rides couldn't have been very pleasant or scenic under the 200 foot ceiling.

The fifth day the fog stood out to sea, temporarily we knew. The plane was gassed in readiness and as the sun filtered through the overlay we took off. The sun shone, the fog stayed out to sea, and our spirits rose as we flew down the rocky coast. Today we might get home. But the fog won.

Joe raced against it for the mouth of Rogue River, which was covered when we reached it. We turned up the river, the fog closing in behind us, covering bars before we could turn back to land on them. At last, about five miles up the river we had enough headway so that Joe could land on a graveled river bar.

The stage was just crossing on the ferry—there were no bridges then. We caught a ride to Gold Beach, the village which had figured so prominently in the Rogue River Indian wars of 1852. Here Joe found another good wide river bar and late that afternoon brought the plane down under the fog and landed near town.

The salmon season was in full swing and fishermen had money to spend. We decided to stay a few days to recoup on our hitherto financially-disasterous trip. First Joe got strips of white cloth to tie on the telephone line which crossed the river, so he could see where it was. He earned sixty or seventy dollars a day for three days, paying up our gas bills. Then one beautiful evening we flew down to Crescent City in just fifty minutes.

But it had taken us thirteen days to fly about two hundred miles. We wrote to Mr. Gorst that we felt any future airmail route should go inland, out of reach of coastal summer fogs.

It had been a mistake to contract to buy the campground. Joe detested cleaning cabins. We didn't have money to fix up the store. Our partner was disappointed in airplane passenger business, which couldn't be extended without extra spare parts. Anyway, winter was coming when there wouldn't be any business.

I was asked to return to my old school up the Chetco River to complete a term when another teacher left. Joe was offered a job driving tractor on a road-grading contract out of Brookings. We decided to accept both offers and turned the campground over to our partner.

My aunt and uncle were away for the winter and their ranch was rented, but we located a tiny log cabin on the banks of the Chetco where we could batch and moved up with a minimum camping outfit.

Within a month after beginning to teach I found that I was

pregnant. I walked two miles to school, my health was excellent and I didn't miss a day during those six and a half months.

Joe drove the old Model T to work. We both put our wages into the campground to pay for new cabins that were being built.

About the first of December Joe was hurt when the tractor hung up on a snag and threw him over the steering wheel. Sharp pain stabbed his side and he couldn't draw a deep breath. He was forced to give up his job.

The company doctor found nothing wrong and wouldn't authorize workman's compensation. At Christmas we went to Ashland to spend the holidays with my family. Here Joe had x-rays which showed broken ribs, with splinters of bone working into the heart area. The claim was finally authorized but we didn't know when it would be paid.

Aunt Edith and Uncle Frank came home and when they saw the dark, cheerless place where we were living they moved us at once up to the ranch. Then it was a delight to come home from school on a rainy evening to a good supper, a fireplace fire, and Aunt Edith's cheery presence.

One of my school families moved away and I finished my term with only two little boys in my student body, in the second and fourth grades.

My wages had gone into the campground, and we got nothing in return. We had made a mistake in buying it, and a worse mistake in taking a partner without a formal, written agreement. We could not come to satisfactory terms, so we turned everything over to him. I hated to give up the few pieces of furniture we had bought, and to lose two years of work in addition to the money we had put in. Today this is a valuable piece of property.

When school was over in late April we took my last check to buy two tickets to Los Angeles on the Southern Pacific. Joe felt he might get a job where he was known, and Dad Barrows had written that he would arrange for the bone operation which Joe must have. With those bone splinters threatening his heart he was almost afraid to move. The doctor agreed to wait for the workmen's compensation money, and if it never came Joe could pay when he got back to work.

Joe's sister, Marjorie, took us in and I stayed at her home in Eagle Rock while Joe recuperated from his successful operation.

Two weeks later he was out making weary rounds of the flying fields on Western Avenue, at Clover Field, and at every branch of the aviation industry around Los Angeles. There were no openings. Good pilots were out of work. Aviation appeared to be on its last legs. No one saw any future in carrying passengers for joy rides.

Now we were really desperate. We didn't have a cent. My baby was nearly due. The workman's compensation money hadn't come. Joe couldn't find work. Would we have to admit defeat and go back to his parents in San Jacinto?

On June 7th Joe cadged a ride with a friend in San Diego. In great excitement he called long distance to tell me he was hired by Ryan Airlines to fly for thirty-five dollars a week.

A job! And flying! He was happy to be back in the air again. And thirty-five dollars a week just then sounded like riches.

That same day an official-looking envelope arrived, containing a compensation check for $450. Joe's hospital bill was paid, his doctor bill was paid, and there was money left for my expected hospital bill.

Our luck had turned at last.

On June 12th, just five days later, my sister-in-law went with me to the hospital in Glendale. Here I spent a nightmarish morning. Mother Barrows arrived from San Jacinto and Joe flew up from San Diego, and by that time I was down in the valley of the shadow. Something was wrong, and I was wheeled into the x-ray room for pictures. I heard whispered consultations in the hall.

About two in the afternoon the doctor, looking grave, came into my room. I remember that it was a hot day, with sun beating in the window. Joe, Mother, and Marjorie were clustered around my bed, all looking worried.

"Everything is wrong," the doctor said frankly. "There is no chance that the baby can be born alive by a normal delivery."

"Not be alive!" It was incredible, I who had been so well, I who had walked four miles every day to school.

"No, and you'd probably die too in attempting to deliver it. There is just one thing to do. We must perform a Caesarean operation at once."

"Will—will the baby be all right then?" I faltered.

"Yes. I'm sure of it."

"Then go ahead."

I had no time to get frightened, although I had only heard of this operation being performed in extreme emergencies. Nurses rushed at me. Almost at once I was on a stretcher being wheeled into the operating room.

Hours later when I fought back to consciousness Joe was hovering over me, grinning from ear to ear.

"It's a lovely little girl. My, she's pretty. I'll bet all the other fathers will be jealous when they have to compare their babies with her. She's the prettiest baby in the nursery, all pink and white instead of red!"

Then he flew back to San Diego to his job and after twelve days in the hospital I convalesced at Marjorie's and Loren's home.

My hospital and doctor bills, with extra for special nurses, came to over five hundred dollars. I was thankful we hadn't known ahead of this emergency expense, during those long weeks when we hadn't even had five dollars—let alone five hundred!

CHAPTER FOUR

Aviation's Awakening Years

Ryan Airlines was one of the oldest established airlines in the west. The planes used were cabin Standards, but a factory was opening to begin production of the first Ryan monoplanes. Joe's brother, Bob, came down from San Jacinto to work in the shops during his summer vacation from high school. He was given charge of a stockroom where tools, equipment and spare parts were stored.

Joe's first important flight for Ryans was a mapping expedition down the Colorado River. He made the trip in a non-stop flight. On this flight he wore a parachute for the first time, and flew for the first time in a monoplane. After the old crates he had always flown—Jennies, Standards or rebuilt hybreds—the swift new monoplane handled like a dream.

When our Margaret Louise, or Margie Lou as we called her, was six weeks old I took her to San Diego. We rented a pleasant little house at Ocean Beach, the nicest home we had yet had. There were plastered walls, a gas range, wicker furniture in the living room. Grandpa Noyes had given the baby a new buggy and she took her naps out of doors. Every afternoon I wheeled her for long walks down to the beach and she thrived in the warm salt air.

Joe used to circle over the house on his return from a flight to Los Angeles and I would go out to wave at him. There was not much work and he spent part of his time repairing motors, washing planes and so on. There were only two pilots employed at that end of the line, one for student instruction and one for passenger flights. One was "Red" Harrigan and the other was "Red" Barrows.

With two raises Joe was now receiving forty-five dollars a week. We were paying our debts and knew how the couple in the old joke felt when they said, "Only two more payments and the baby is ours."

In November a wealthy eastern woman chartered a plane to fly around the state of California and Joe was to be her pilot. He flew up to Los Angeles to meet her and took Margie Lou and me along. This was the baby's first airplane ride, taken just before she was five months old. I put cotton in her ears and wrapped her warmly as the old cabin Standards did not have glass in the windows and

25

there was a strong draft through them. When I lifted her from the plane on Angeles Mesa airport attendants clustered around, exclaiming about such a small baby having flown.

One woman, hearing that I had taken her up, remarked, "It's plain she doesn't love her baby much. It's bad enough for her to let her husband fly, but as for taking that poor defenseless baby! She must want to kill it!"

The old Standard which Joe flew on this trip was later shipped to Hawaii for use by Martin Jensen in the Islands.

Shortly before Christmas Joe was called for an unusual bit of flying. A highway in Mexico had been washed out by slides and the Tia Juana saloons were unable to get their holiday supply of beer from the Mexicali breweries. Ryan Airlines sent three airplanes across the border to haul beer.

The pilots and mechanics camped in the heat of the desert near Mexicali. The opposite end of the flight was made in snow banks at the top of the mountain directly above, where the kegs were unloaded and transferred to trucks. The flight back was made in about four minutes empty, but the loaded planes had to circle for half an hour to gain the altitude necessary to land on the mountain.

The exposure gave Joe rheumatism. He landed in snow minutes after leaving the blazing desert heat. His feet were wet all the time. The men also suffered from indigestion caused by the highly seasoned Mexican food they ate.

One day on the streets of Mexicali a soldier approached Joe.

"You aviator?" asked the soldier.

"Yes."

"I shoot at you!" announced the soldier.

"What?"

"You fly over our fort?" the soldier wanted to make sure he was talking to the right person.

"Yes."

"Well, Americans say soldiers can not hit airplanes with rifles. When you fly over we shoot at you, try to hit you. We not hit you yet."

Startled, Joe began flying around the fort instead of over it.

On New Year's Day an earthquake destroyed the Mexicali brewery and the flights of "operation beer lift" were automatically terminated.

In January Joe went on a demonstration flight with a new Ryan monoplane, north to San Francisco and across into the San Joaquin Valley. Soon winter rains made the few fields too muddy to use so he and the salesman started back toward San Diego. Rain was coming down in sheets and weather reports indicated that it would continue. But Joe hadn't been home in six weeks and he decided to fly through.

Visibility was almost zero-zero. By flying low, following highway lights, Joe kept his direction. Suddenly a sheet of rain blotted out the lights. He leveled off to land, instinctively remembering a field somewhere near which he had located during his routine flights to Los Angeles. In darkness he made a safe landing. Daylight showed the field to be full of holes which would have been hard to miss in bright sunlight. When the plane was flown out, one man walked ahead to point out the holes while the pilot taxied.

While Joe was in San Francisco he had met men interested in establishing flying schools and airlines. There was then no real field anywhere around the Bay region and, compared with the aviation industry in the southern part of the state, aviation was only in its infancy farther north. Joe felt it was a good time, and an excellent location, for launching a business of his own. The wealthy woman whom he had taken on a charter flight offered to loan him a thousand dollars to start a company of his own.

He told me about the possibilities of aviation around San Francisco Bay, about the business he wanted to develop, and about his offer of financial backing.

"But you've just been raised to sixty dollars a week—that's big wages," I objected. "And we have another baby coming. That will be another five hundred dollar doctor and hospital bill. I don't want to move. I don't want the insecurity of having no steady salary coming in."

"Oh, I'll be back on a salary in a few weeks," he promised.

He told me that a young mail pilot had just bought a Ryan monoplane and was then at the factory overseeing its construction. This mail pilot was planning some foolish thing like trying to fly the Atlantic Ocean in a single-motored land plane. His name was Charles Lindbergh.

The projected flight interested Joe—and terrified me!

"I tell you, this is going to be a great year in aviation. And I want to be in on it."

I couldn't stand in his way so, reluctantly, I agreed to the move. We took the train up to Oakland.

In San Francisco Joe had met a former acquaintance who had been in the barn-storming business and had failed. But he had valuable experience in aviation and in salesmanship, and a wide acquaintance. Together they began developing details of a projected company.

Joe's ideas had been modest—a small flying school, one or two ships for taxi work, and gradual expansion as business increased. But the other man broadened these original plans and they soon decided to incorporate for half a million dollars, dreamed of twenty planes on scheduled airlines which would link the whole coast in a network of routes. They worked out charts of rates for passengers and freight to every town in the west. Lines of flight were mapped, costs of operation and estimated returns were figured. And neither of them had a dime. Nor were there any airports at most of these towns.

Airplanes were landing on the filled-in tide flats of Bay Farm Island, in the East Bay area near Alameda, so Joe decided that should be our base.

We looked for a furnished house in Alameda, but there was nothing we could afford. Finally, out on Bay Farm Island, we found an unfurnished bungalow we could rent for twenty-five dollars a month. It was in a Jerry-built subdivision but was new and clean. There were hardwood floors, a built-in breakfast nook and a bathroom with a recessed tub.

Eighty dollars of our precious capital went for furniture and we moved in. I remember how every cent of the eighty dollars was stretched. The kitchen got a tiny three-burner gas range for ten dollars second-hand. At Montgomery Ward on a time payment plan we bought a grass rug and a three-piece wicker set upholstered in black and bright orange. I bought a gate-leg table for $2.98 and painted it orange. Cretonne curtains made the room gay and cheerful. A dollar bookstand completed the living room furniture.

One bedroom held only a second-hand crib for Margie Lou. For the other we got a bed and dresser which had been slightly scratched so they were on sale. The rest of the money went for a coil spring and as good a mattress as we could afford. About this time I also got a set of dishes as a premium for subscribing to the Oakland Tribune—before this we had used odds and ends from the dime stores.

Joe and his partner walked from office to office in San Francisco and Oakland trying to finance their projected business. Everywhere they met rebuffs. People did not believe aviation had a commercial future; it was a sport in the category of speed-boat racing. Discouraged, they engaged a promoter who talked them into believing he was a wizard at money getting. Together they invested a borrowed thousand dollars in him, renting and furnishing an office and giving him their bond of good faith—all on the strength of a handsomely printed booklet describing his self-admitted power to extract money from hard-headed business men.

One day Joe found the office locked. The furniture company took back the furniture which had not been paid for. The promoter was gone, and so was the thousand dollars. We found later that he was apprehended in Los Angeles conducting some illegal promotion scheme there—probably on our money.

The partner lost interest. He found an engineer who was designing a new plane and told us it would be cheaper to build our own planes than to buy them. After they were tested and put into quantity production airlines could be started using our own airplanes. Think of the publicity!

In the meantime we had to eat. Our money was gone. A baby was coming. Joe took a temporary job driving the Bay Farm Island bus afternoons and nights. That left him his mornings to continue searching for a man with faith enough in aviation to "grub-stake" a pilot.

At that time, in May of 1927, there were only a few airplanes on the Oakland side of the bay, mostly old Jennies. The pilots had a few students and on Sunday afternoons carried passengers. They took off from the filled-in tide flats. There was no inspection or supervision of either planes or pilots. A student who had just soloed started carrying passengers and crashed with two. Another homemade plane fell apart in the air and the pilot was killed. Planes took off directly over cars. There were constant casualties, all played up with headlines in the newspapers.

But over the nation wonderful things were happening. MacCready and Kelly flew over Dayton, Ohio for 36 hours and 5 minutes in April, 1925. They also made a nonstop flight across the continent in 26 hours and 50 minutes, using 737 gallons of gasoline and 40 gallons of oil.

Mr. Gorst had started his Pacific Air Transport carrying mail up and down the coast—through the inland valleys. He had called Joe long distance to offer him a job when the first flights were made, but as Joe was then working for Ryans he had to refuse.

Then in May Charles Lindbergh, flying a Ryan monoplane, took off from New York and landed in Paris.

I was standing on a corner in Alameda, my arms full of groceries, waiting for Joe to come along in the rickety Bay Farm Island bus, when boys began screaming 'extras' on the streets. When Joe saw the papers I thought he would weep. Here he was, tied to the ground, driving an old bus, when aviation history was being made, when he wanted to help make it.

Nothing had stirred the nation like this flight.

Almost overnight the tide flats were transformed into an airport. A runway was graded and conditioned for Maitland and Hegenberger's flight to Hawaii. I carried Margie out to see their plane take off about seven one morning, passing sluggishly scarcely twenty feet above the roof of our cottage. This was the first flight across the Pacific.

But on the east coast Chamberlain and Levine took off for Germany, and Byrd and his party landed on the coast of France.

Every aviator in the west tried frantically to get a plane ready when Mr. Dole posted his offer of a $25,000 prize for the first civilian plane to fly to Honolulu. Joe got a seaman's guide to the islands and began studying it. When he said he thought he could get a backer and a plane for the flight—a Corsair which Dick Grace later wrecked in the Islands—I began to get worried. The preparations all seemed so hasty. The planes weren't properly equipped. The pilots didn't know navigation.

A Captain Doty offered Joe a chance to fly for him for two weeks while the Captain did a period of active duty at Crissy Field and Joe gladly quit the bus driving job to be in the air again.

While I was in the hospital for the advent of our son, Frank—my second Caesarean operation—Ernie Smith flew to one of the Hawaiian Islands. The papers were full of the impending Dole race. Joe had reluctantly decided not to try it—he had only $690 insurance and two babies.

Commercial pilots were banned from the airport as planes were readied for the race. Bob, Joes's brother, came up to see the excitement, quitting his summer job at the Ryan airplane factory. He found work helping gas two of the planes, the Woolarac (which won the race) and the Oklahoma. Every night he went out to stand guard over the gas drums and most of the day he was also at the field, afraid he might miss something.

On the morning of the race we drove to the airport in a borrowed car. The traffic was dense and, early as we were, we were forced into the third row of cars. Many people had camped there all night in order to have advantageous positions. I fixed a bed for the baby in the bottom of the car, and Margie Lou sat on top of it with us until she got sleepy and took a nap inside.

The spectators were gay. Peanut and sandwich or program vendors gave the aspect of a carnival to the scene. Bets were being made freely. Joe had attended a flier's banquet the week before where a lottery was formed and lucky tickets given out. Whoever held the winning ticket—there was one for each plane entered—would win $750 if the plane won the race. He would win $1500 if that plane was the only entrant to reach Hawaii. Joe held one of the lucky tickets and we saw the plane on which it was drawn, Norman Goddard's El Encanto, waver down the runway and crash at the end. Goddard's and our chances were gone in less than two minutes.

Amid a din of motors the planes began to warm up. We saw the purple and orange Oklahoma pushed into first position and watched the checkered flag go up. At the end of the field ambulances and fire engines were stationed, grim reminders of the innate dangers of this spectacle. Our excitement was great as we climbed to the car top to watch the Travel Air go down the runway, but it had not yet reached fever pitch.

"He can't get the tail up," cries and comments sounded all around us.

"He's got it up."

"He's off."

"No, he's down again."

"He'll neve make it with that heavy load."

"He's off. He's off."

And he was off the ground at last.

Goddard's plane toppled over on one wing at the end of the runway. Martin Jensen in the "Aloha" got off slowly and climbed as slowly, taking no chances. He was not more than twenty feet high as far away as we could see the orange plane winging across the Bay, toward the Golden Gate, toward the Pacific and the distant islands. Martin Jensen might have won the race, so commentators said, had his navigator known modern methods of navigation instead of the old maritime system which required 'shooting the sun' just at noon and which took about two hours for computations to be made.

Art Goebel in the Woolarac, another Travel Air monplane, made a good take-off and continued straight to Hawaii and fame.

Major Irving, in a Breese monoplane, tried twice to take off, was successful on the second attempt but couldn't keep the plane in the air and finally crashed. The beautiful "Golden Eagle", a Lockheed with Jack Frost at the controls, was never heard from after it passed the Farralone Islands.

Augie Pedlar, with two passengers, one "Miss Doran" for whom the plane was named, made a pretty take-off in a red, white and blue Buhl. In two hours he was back and landed with a full gas load to make a minor repair. Without taking on a gallon more of gas, he started out again to his fate. The plane in the first place had such a small margin of gas that the inspectors were dubious about passing it.

Captain Erwin came back in an hour with the fuselage covering of his Swallow monoplane flapping. Two days later he took off with the heaviest load that a plane of that size had ever lifted, and went west to search for the missing "Golden Eagle" and "Miss Doran". During the night his radio sent the words, "We are in a tail spin, Now we are in another—" Then silence. Two months later his young widow gave birth to a baby who never knew its courageous father.

The great air tragedy ended. Sixteen planes had entered at first.

One crashed into Point Loma at San Diego on its way north and two men were killed. Another entrant was killed in Los Angeles. A triplane went into the Bay across from Bay Farm Island when the pilot swerved to avoid hitting parked cars on the Airport Way. Others withdrew or were ruled out because they could not pass the requirements, which were not half rigid enough. Six planes finally rose into the air and started for Hawaii. Two reached the islands. The Oklahoma came back, and the Dallas Spirit was lost two days after the race.

"It is only a question of time," Joe wrote then, prophetically, "before we will have established airlines over the oceans, lines flying with as much safety and schedule as the airmail lines."

He didn't know that eleven years later he would be flying across the Pacific on one of these routes.

Last fall when I flew on a Pan American Airways plane from Portland to Honolulu, an easy five hour flight with lunch en route, it seemed a long time ago that I watched the Dole race for the Hawaiian Islands. My plane continued on to Tokyo, and it was still daylight when we landed.

After this tragedy, aviation business slumped. Joe had taken the Waco agency but he didn't have a Waco to demonstrate.

My brother, Frank, had come to San Francisco to seek his fortune and was working in a chain grocery store putting cans on the shelves. He was let out and came over to starve with us. From the middle of August until the first of October we had practically no money. We had often been broke, but at least up in Crescent City we could eat groceries from the store. This situation was more desperate than our customary poverty.

On two Sundays in seven weeks Joe had a chance to fly for some other pilot and made a few dollars, enough to pay the rent and the milk bill. During seven weeks we lived on less than eighty dollars, including two month's rent, gas, lights and water—and we didn't go in debt. Near our house was a field in which Swiss chard was growing wild, and we ate Swiss chard until I never wanted to see any again—rich as it may be in vitamins. We bought a hundred pound sack of potatoes for 90¢ and I baked them, boiled them, fried them and made potato soup. For seven weeks our diet was principally Swiss chard and potatoes.

Then a pilot went on a prolonged spree and his partner called Joe to instruct his students. Among them was an elderly doctor who became interested in Joe and offered to buy a Waco, letting Joe use it and pay for it as it earned money. The next day a young rancher bought another Waco. After its delivery the rancher, a student pilot, crashed the plane in the Bay. He sold it back to Joe after it had been in salt water overnight, for the commission Joe had earned. We borrowed money to repair it.

Now Joe was able to get a few students of his own.

Frank had been unable to find work. He had finished high school and attended the newly re-activated Southern Oregon Normal School at Ashland—at least until basketball season was over—but his only work experience had been on Dad's ranch and in the family-operated sawmill. Living as he was in an aviator's home, it was inevitable that he should become interested in flying. Joe offered to teach him, giving him board and room in exchange for services around the field, and flying time when convenient.

So he took his time, a few minutes here and there, and soloed with four hours and fifteen minutes of instruction. On my birthday in February he phoned me and said, "Well, I've soloed and I'm still alive."

Four years later, when I soloed up in Alaska I wrote him and began my letter with the same sentence.

In July he earned his limited commercial license and could carry passengers around the field. In October he got his transport license. Yes, by 1928 pilots were being licensed.

Joe was away from the field on the day the inspector gave the first examinations, or his license number would have been under 100. As it was, his was No. 255. Frank's the next year was in the 2000's, and when I got mine four years later it was over 20,000. So fast had aviation grown.

The Fairchild Aerial Surveys, for whom Joe did some flying, asked him to recommend a mapping pilot as one of theirs was ill. Joe was busy and recommended Frank. Frank was only twenty then, had never flown a cabin plane, and had never been up at a three mile elevation. He had, however, done considerable compass flying under Joe's rigorous cross-country training. His pictures were perfect, each strip overlapping exactly. For two months he flew at Bakersfield on a mapping job; later he air-mapped Yosemite, and in May went to Canada to fly a pontoon plane on a job. Eighteen months after he soloed he was one of three accredited Fairchild Aerial Survey pilots in California. (Joe was one of the others.) Before he was of age he was drawing a salary of a hundred dollars a week.

But that was later. This was still 1928, a year of trial and errors. There were no precedents to follow in building aviation business.

Joe rented an uptown office, had a business manager and a stenographer and ordered expensive letterhead stationery, business cards, and advertisements in papers and aviation magazines. He named his company the "Pacific and Atlantic Airways." That sounded big, but it was too big. We had two planes, one of those a crashed one. Finally the name changed to

"Pacific Coast Air Service." A commercial artist drew a red bird which was painted on the planes and decorated the letterheads.

Joe tested a new motor in the rebuilt Waco, which was a success. Articles came out about the motor, but Joe's name wasn't mentioned—and he was supposed to get publicity for his work. Again he learned about business, and that verbal agreements didn't equal a name on a dotted line.

Our little son, Frank, was nicknamed Teddy. For a year after his birth I was not well. During the fall I grew thinner and weaker until at Christmastime I was spending most of the time in bed. Joe and Frank bathed the babies, did the never-ending washing, fixed bottles and kept house.

Again we were broke, but wanted a little Christmas for Margie Lou. Joe bought a little tree and a red chair for 75¢. My cousin in Berkeley had invited us for Christmas dinner but I was too weak to make the long bus and streetcar ride and we didn't have money enough for fares anyway.

Christmas Eve I was in bed, too weak to hold up my head. Vaguely I heard Joe and Frank moving furniture, and thought I heard one of them on the roof. About ten o'clock I suddenly heard the strains of a Christmas carol. My men came with beaming faces to carry me out to the living room. They had been installing a radio. Someway they had saved enough money to make a down payment on a battery set for my Christmas present. Of course it was extravagant, but confined as I was with ill health and two babies, they thought it justifiable. "Hyacinths to feed the soul" sometimes mean more than continual counting of pennies.

Business improved in the spring. Joe made a successful bid on Forest Patrol flying, a new field. He acquired another plane and rented a Fairchild. With this equipment, a mechanic, and an extra pilot, plus a helper or two, we had quite a personnel. But the city office expenses drained off our income.

When Sir Charles Kingsford-Smith flew the Southern Cross to Australia, the navigator, Captain Voortmeyer, who had prepared the charts, recommended Joe as a relief pilot. Such publicity would have put him several years up in his climb in aviation. But the babies were so young— When I landed on the huge Kingsford-Smith Airport at Sydney the first time I regretted Joe's lost opportunity. Those early day aviators shouldn't have been hampered by family responsibilities.

During the next two years Joe was seldom home. Taxi business was good. He might fly an eloping couple to Reno, a movie actor to a summer resort, a party of rich ranchers into the hills on a hunting trip. And he was on twenty-four hour call from the Forest Service. I kept clean clothes ready constantly so I could pack his bag at a moment's notice.

We moved into Alameda where it was easier for me to shop with two babies in a baby buggy, or to get to the library for books which were usually my sole companions in the evening after the children were asleep.

Once my sister-in-law, Marjorie, came to visit and offered to stay with the children so I could make a Forest Patrol flight with Joe. We flew north toward the mountains I loved. I stayed in Shasta City while Joe flew his patrol, enjoying the mountain air and the delicious water. In the city one forgets how good cold water can be. At five o'clock Joe finished his patrol over a fire burning in the isolated Trinity Alps and we decided to go on to Oregon for the night. At dusk we crossed the Siskiyous and landed at Medford. This plane was too fast to land on an Ashland hillside pasture where Joe had landed the old Jenny. Art Starbuck, a pilot for Pacific Air Transport, drove us to town from the airport.

I telephoned to Ashland and my father and my four sisters came down to see us, my little sisters who were growing up so fast. Also my high school chum, Violet, arrived. It was good to see them—I hadn't realized how lonely I really was. Next morning we were off at daybreak and watched the sun rise behind Mt. Shasta. The flight was beautiful but I nearly froze in the open cockpit. We landed at Oakland and were home for breakfast. This was the first time I had left the children overnight.

Joe flew seven days a week—Sundays were busiest. He tried to pay off debts and to get ahead of the staggering burden of overhead expenses. During fire season he was home about two nights out of seven weeks, usually coming in from patrol flights to get a meal and clean clothes.

Fairchild Aerial Surveys hired him for a six weeks mapping job between Bakersfield and Sacramento, flying at an altitude of 18,000 feet. This is difficult, exacting work. The pilot flies by compass to keep his strips straight. They must overlap exactly and each strip must correspond with the last one flown. The work is tiring at this altitude, without oxygen, hard on the heart and the ears. But it paid a hundred dollars a week, and that was 'top wages' then, except in the airmail.

At the Los Angeles Air Show Joe was offered the Fairchild dealership. He sold a Wasp-motored Fairchild to a mining company in Alaska and went to New York to take delivery, taking Frank along to give him cross-country experience. They were like two children in their anticipation of a trip to NEW YORK—in capitals! This was Joe's first transcontinental flight.

He also acquired a lease on some tide lands in Alameda near the ferry slip and planned to build a centrally-located airport. This lease was lost to people with more money and more influence. To me there was irony in the big money talk as we had just reached the point where we could afford our first car since my old Model T, a new Model A Ford. Joe was now taking out a salary of $50 a week from the company and for the first time since Ryans I had some security. I even went to look at a piece of land in the Oakland Hills with the idea of having a house built. I wonder what that lot is worth today!

Eventually Joe checked the books of the Pacific Coast Air Service and found that he was losing money every month. All his seven days a week of earnings had kept up an expensive office, a stenographer, a business manager, advertising and so on. The office was moved to the airport. I typed any necessary letters and the overhead was drastically reduced.

An automobile dealer in San Francisco wanted to come in on the Fairchild dealership so once again Joe took a partner. In December they went to the Chicago Air Show and stayed at the Blackstone Hotel—more expensive than the three dollar rooms we used to rent up along the coast.

That same winter I had the worst scare I had ever had during my years as an aviator's wife. Joe and Frank took two planes to Ely, Nevada, to an airport dedication service. Each had a passenger or two, a mechanic, ticket seller and parachute jumper. Harry Blunt, a Washington state rancher who was just learning to fly, went with Frank as a mechanic, and Joe had Walter Hall, the parachute jumper, with him.

Monday Joe had an important appointment but he didn't return. Mother Barrows had undergone a critical operation and her condition was serious. We were concerned about her. I wired Ely, to find that Joe had left the day before. At midnight a San Francisco paper called to tell me they had heard that Joe had crashed in the mountains in Nevada in a snow storm. Next day the radio gave out bulletins that he was missing. In Los Angeles the family tried to keep Mother from guessing that anything was wrong.

This was Frank's first long cross-country flight alone and I was also alarmed about him. From Monday till Friday morning I didn't hear a word. Joe had landed during a snowstorm near a sheepherder's cabin and sat there comfortably listening to the radio broadcasting that he was missing. When the snow stopped long enough for him to fly to the nearest town the telegraph office was closed for the night. Only an aviator's wife knows what those nights of worry are like; sleepless nights of picturing a plane crashed on a snowy hillside, injured men, exploding gas tanks. No wonder gray hairs come early!

36

In the spring of 1929 Joe had to make another trip to New York. He was going to fly an FC2 Fairchild back to the factory on Long Island to have a new motor installed. He asked me to go with him. I couldn't have been more excited!

CHAPTER FIVE

Expanding Horizons

Mother Barrows said she would be glad to keep the children and I hired a girl to stay with her. I had some misgivings about going so far away and knew I would be criticized for leaving Margie Lou and Teddy. But a trip to NEW YORK—again in capitals!

Air baggage must be light so I was allowed to take very few clothes—I didn't have many anyway. For the first time in my life I shopped for an entire new outfit. The basic part of it was a three piece wool jersey suit which didn't muss or wrinkle and which proved a wise purchase for traveling. The suit was brown with an orange sweater. A tan polo coat served for all purposes. Then I bought a brown chiffon dress for dinner and evenings which could be hung in the bathroom where steam would take out its wrinkles. Two pairs of shoes and a tan straw 'cloche' hat completed the wardrobe.

We flew to Los Angeles to leave the children there with their grandparents. Dad Barrows was no longer in San Jacinto but was conductor on the Santa Fe crack train, The Chief, going out to Needles. Margie Lou was nearly three years old and Teddy was almost twenty months.

On an April afternoon we took off from the American Aircraft Field on Angeles Mesa directly over a herd of cattle grazing at the end of the runway.

Since today one can fly across the continent in a few hours, I will go into some detail about a transcontinental flight in 1929. One of the great joys to flying then was the fact that we never lost contact with earth. Today in a pressurized cabin the passenger is above the clouds all the way, at 35,000 feet altitude, and sees the earth only on takeoffs and landings. Then we followed railroads and highways and rivers as navigational aids. We saw the country.

Below were the sprawled streets of the city, from the hills to the fringe of oil derricks wetting their feet in the western ocean. Over orange groves, over Mt. Rubidoux with a peak surmounted by a cross. The San Jacinto Mountains and beyond them the desert. Palm Springs wasn't yet a fashionable resort. Barren, saw-tooth ridges, rocks swept bare of earth and vegetation, desert sands drifted in ripples—gray and pink, fading into blue, lavender and purple in the distance. The Colorado River was a chocolate-colored ribbon snaking through the sand.

Phoenix, set amidst green, irrigated fields. We landed for the night at "Sky Harbor", a splendid field with buildings of Aztec design and with friendly, enterprising attendants. A purple, unfamiliar dusk fell while we waited for a taxi and the clear air had a fascinating tang.

In Arizona we saw the importance of life-giving water. Irrigation ditches held back the desert, with sand and sage and greasewood beyond them. An ancient cliff dwelling clung to a pass in the hills. The Rio Grande, winding along the international border. We landed in El Paso in a wind so strong attendants ran out to hold down the plane.

Our taxi driver wore a ten gallon hat. In the hotel lobby were dusty, windburned tourists, men in flannels, cowboys, ranchers with brown faces and high boots, bell boys in Spanish style costumes with flaring trousers and scarlet sashes.

We crossed the Rio Grande on an International bridge beneath which a little boy bathed naked in the muddy water. Juarez was a sleepy Mexican town, distinctly different from Tia Juana's sordid commercialism. Along residential streets we saw bullet holes in the plastered walls.

"There has been a revolution down this way, hasn't there?" we asked.

"Yes, the Federal soldiers moved in just yesterday. The rebels are still shooting at the edge of town, out behind some box cars."

The restaurant we chose served excellent food but was almost empty.

"Isn't this tourist season?" I asked the waiter.

"Yes, but Americans are afraid to cross the border now on account of the revolution. See the bullet hole in that transom over the door?" I looked at the shattered glass pane. "That was made yesterday."

Away early for a long day over sand and sagebrush. A landing for gas at Dryden on a deserted army field. The lone attendant said his chief diversion was shooting at jack rabbits. More desert, and then ranches, clumps of woodland. Kelly and Duncan Fields at the edge of San Antonio and a landing at Windburn Field with criss-crossing runways white against the green grass. This beautiful field was colorful with a black and yellow T.A.T. plane, a silver Ryan, a red Waco, and an orange Monoprep resting on the green.

East again over fields and woods crazy-quilted together. Rice paddies in standing water—too bad Texas can't distribute its water more evenly. The Brazos River. I always sat with a map in my lap and traced our route as we flew. Houston ahead in the center of a tree-dotted plane.

The airport was ten miles from the city, $2.50 by taxi. Poor service, poor business here as judged by a sign advertising rides for a dollar. Wildflowers in the grass, roses climbing fences, fireflies lighting the bushes.

That evening we attended a movie with a sound track. It was "Show Boat." I heard the song, "Old Man River" for the first time and it put me in a proper mood to see the Mississippi on the morrow.

Next morning Galveston Bay, Sabine Lake and south, through the haze, the Gulf of Mexico. Rice fields. Then a flash of waters, 'old man river'. At first I was disappointed; I had expected it to be at least as wide as San Francisco Bay. But it grew as we descended. In a bend was New Orleans with Lake Pontchartrain gleaming beyond. The airport was inaccessible, west of the river and twenty miles from the city. We waited a precious hour and a half for a taxi.

Quickly we deposited our bags at a hotel and went sightseeing—to the Vieux Caree with its mellowed old houses, fretted iron balconies, old cemeteries, the Cabildo in Jackson Square, a banana boat unloading at a dock. Then Antoine's for dinner for food such as I had never eaten before.

A four-thirty wakening was not glamorous. The ferry boat was filthy and I was aghast at signs 'For White Only'. The river was high and laden with silt.

Joe had worked out a compass course and pencilled it on the maps, and he never deviated a mile from it as he crossed unknown country. He was one of the first pilots to learn to use instruments.

In southern Mississippi I saw an alligator lying on a sand bar beside a yellow stream which flowed through swamps. Trees were festooned with Spanish moss. Gas at Montgomery, Alabama where two or three old hangars stood at the edge of a field. No one was busy. There wasn't even a restroom. Off over red soil and unpainted shacks which were gray and weathered.

A rough runway and a bumpy landing at Atlanta. Field attendants were playing horseshoes and couldn't be bothered to service our plane. We waited for a rattling taxi to take us along streets with beautiful trees and flowers but with unkempt buildings with broken steps, lawns that needed mowing, and people sitting in porch swings. At what was recommended as the best hotel we had a poor meal with cold coffee and soggy potatoes. The restroom was actually dirty. The taxi driver charged $3.50 to take us back to the field. Our stop here, with the drive to town and back and our lunch, had cost us $16.25 and wasted three precious, daylight hours.

More red soil and rough red hills to Spartanburg, South Carolina which was picturesque from the air. The field attendants were hospitable and the hotel clean and comfortable. Our dinner was delicious and a dignified waiter in a swallowtail coat presided over our table. Mice played on the floor; the waiter said they were tame.

Sunday it rained in sheets so we stayed over. Next morning the air was rough and the horizon toward the Blue Mountains was hazy. We lunched at Richmond, landing at Byrd Field and driving to town along a road where a Civil War battle was fought, a country road down which McClellan's troops had marched. Strange to picture war in such a peaceful setting but on the airport cadets were training for a future one. Across the James River, past the white church where Patrick Henry asked for liberty or death, and past the building which had been the capitol of the Confederacy.

North over the Potomac and our nation's capitol. At our altitude I could pick out Mt. Vernon. I saw the spire of the Washington Monument, the Capitol dome, the Arlington cemetery, all familiar through photographs. We flew on over Annapolis, Baltimore, Chesapeake Bay, Philadelphia, Trenton, the Delaware River where Washington crossed amid grinding cakes of ice. Ahead was the Atlantic Ocean—we had actually spanned the continent.

Manhattan's skyscrapers jutted up through the gathering dusk and the city smoke. We came down over the Statue of Liberty, over steamers in the harbor, over Long Island, to a landing on the Fairchild Field at Farmingdale.

Our time in the air had been approximately thirty-seven hours, and we had flown about 3,750 miles from Oakland and had been seven days on the way.

Dick Depew, one of America's first fliers and a member of Early Birds (pilots who flew before World War One), took us into the city. Up Fifth Avenue amid speeding taxis, crowds, the rumble of elevated trains, the noise and traffic of early evening. New York.

While Joe worked I diligently went sight-seeing, trying to find the glamour of that huge city. I rode on buses, I took sight-seeing tours, and I longed for the open spaces of Texas. My heart ached for ghetto children playing in crowded streets lined with pushcarts and with laundry hung overhead. April was still wintry and I was cold in my light coat when chill winds blew down the canyon-like streets. And how dirty those streets were. Wind picked up dust, torn newspapers, filth and swished it in the faces of passersby. I always had a cinder in my eye.

Our hotel room seemed to shake with the whizzing of the express elevators, the roar of trains and subways beneath the ground, the clamor of taxis and traffic. I woke every morning with a headache.

We went back to Washington where Joe was trying to sell the Persian legation a fleet of Fairchilds to take to Persia. And for a week I explored Washington—the Smithsonian Museum, the Congressional Library, the dignified government buildings and lovely old houses. I took sight-seeing tours, which are wonderful for strangers in a city, and thrilled to walk around Mount Vernon.

Later, as Joe would spend some time in New York getting the Fairchild overhauled, I took a train to Boston. Sight of placid ponds, old square houses, and the stone fences of New England gave me a feeling of familiarity. My mother was a Vermonter, but that didn't explain my sense of belonging. I loved New England at once.

More sight-seeing in Boston and Concord, steeping myself in history. Then another train ride to Nashua, New Hampshire to visit Grandpa Noyes's older brother, great-uncle Reverend Warren Noyes, for sixty years an ordained minister in the Congregational Church. He and Aunt Mary lived in a huge old house with heirloom furniture and booklined walls. Another great-uncle came from Manchester to see me and regaled me with anecdotes of Grandpa's early life. He and I made plans to go to Vermont to see my mother's birthplace but that night Joe phoned to say that the plane was ready and I must return to New York.

On a June morning we left Long Island, bound for the Golden Gate. The Statue of Liberty had its arm raised as if in farewell. I wasn't sorry to leave. I didn't belong in crowded areas where anything west of Hoboken was 'out west'.

Within a hundred miles we were over farms and woodlands. The Susquehanna River wound below, peaceful and lovely between rolling hills like soft green and brown pillows with trees for raised embroidery. A sudden rain squall brought us down at Sunbury, and that night I heard boys clattering along the street on horseback instead of the thunder of subways, trains and elevators. Here were old, old houses, solid and picturesque. Sunbury was incorporated in 1779.

The next day we followed the airmail route, seeing emergency fields or beacons below us. This was coal country with grayish heaps of refuse, excavations, black smoke. Cleveland was covered with smoke and haze so we saw only the large airport with modern hangars and administration buildings, a busy place.

The plane bucked headwinds all morning. Chicago was also wreathed in smoke so we saw little. A Fairchild man took us to lunch and told exciting tales of gangsters who shot his wings full of holes over this same, quiet-seeming suburb.

On west into stronger headwinds and squally rain. Across the Mississippi into Iowa over prosperous farms with white houses and big red barns. Visibility decreased and rain lashed the windows. Joe dropped lower, hedge-hopping, to find our way. Chickens and calves were frightened as we roared overhead. In a barnyard a cow kicked over the farmer who was milking her and he shook his clenched fist up at us. At last we came out over Council Bluffs and saw the yellow Missouri and beyond it the American Legion Airport at Omaha. Here Joe landed, weary from fighting headwinds after fourteen hours in the air.

All night it rained and the taxi detoured in the morning to get to the field, sliding on slippery streets. We worried about a take-off but a friendly black field attendant assured Joe, "You-all stay on the runway and you'll be O.K. But if you-all dash out into that theah mud you'se gwine to hab trouble."

The ground didn't permit any dashing. We taxied off the concrete apron into a sea of mud which splattered the wings as we moved forward.

Nebraska looked prosperous. The Platte was running bankful. The country below took on a familiar appearance. I had spent my childhood on these prairies and remembered the white schoolhouses, the grain elevators, the stacks of straw left behind the threshing machines. Cottonwoods and willows still grew along the Platte as they had when we drove into Sterling from the homestead. I had a memory of myself sitting on the front seat of the buckboard as Dad whipped up his fast white horses to make a good entrance into town.

It was only forty smiles or so to our old homestead, south across into Colorado, but Joe didn't deviate from his compass course so we entered Wyoming. Cheyenne looked new and raw after the weathered old houses of Sunbury.

We ate lunch in a restaurant decorated with Hawaiian pictures, here in the heart of the west. Why don't cities capitalize on their own environments, their own local history, scenery and products? That would be much more interesting than imported pseudo-atmosphere.

Over cattle country and the ground rising toward the Rockies. A cowboy on a white horse waved his sombrero at us. Ahead were the grand, imposing ranges down the backbone of the continent where white mountains blended with white clouds. Into Utah over snow-capped mountains, tree-bordered streams, ranch buildings, purple sage. I asked Joe to sell the airplane and buy a ranch—I was positively homesick for a horse to ride. Through a pass with the altimeter showing 11,000 elevation, and out over Salt Lake valley with the great lake shimmering under the sun. We circled over university buildings, over the State Capitol and the Mormon temple and tabernacle and then landed on a white, salt plain.

Weather reports were bad next morning. The mail planes were grounded at Reno, unable to cross the Sierras. We needed no more excuse to detour to Los Angeles to pick up the children.

South we flew across Utah and Nevada, over sagebrush and rocks. Below were jagged hills, not prim little Pennsylvania pillows. This land was wild and lovely with red rocks and red canyons. Lavendar haze hung over the far mountains. Las Vegas at lunch time, a raw, new town a long way from the honky-tonk city of today. Our plane wheels stirred up soft sand and choking white dust.

Back over San Bernardino county, the largest county in the United States—so I've been told. What a state California is, combining beaches and Salton Seas, orange groves and redwood forests, deserts and snow-capped mountains, palms and pines. The desert and sage and yucca gave way to orange groves, then to cities.

We completed our flight home with two new passengers. Margie Lou sat in her daddy's lap to help him fly. Teddy was a little airsick and not sure he liked airplanes, sleeping most of the three hour flight to Oakland.

Our homeward trip had taken only four and a half days, from New York City to Sunbury, Sunbury to Omaha, Omaha to Salt Lake City, Salt Lake City to Los Angeles, and up to Oakland. We had flown over twenty-nine states, had entered Mexico at Juarez, and had spent a week in the District of Columbia. Our air time was approximately 67 hours from the Pacific to the Atlantic and back again.

After our return Joe moved his planes and operations across the Bay to Mills Field, south of San Francisco, and we rented a pleasant house in San Bruno. I got a new rug to replace the worn out straw one, and traded the wicker set in on an upholstered davenport and chair, a reading lamp and an end table. Now our house was like the rest of the great 'middle class'—without personality or individuality.

I also attained the luxury of having a woman come twice a week to wash and clean and my weary back was rested after three years of washing diapers by hand.

Joe, quite by accident, entered the Cleveland Air races that year. He had two passengers for a charter flight to Cleveland. His plane was heavily loaded with built-in landing lights and moving picture apparatus. But at the last minute there were only five entrants from Oakland and the prize money would not be awarded unless there were six, so two hours before starting time Joe registered.

We were surprised to hear that he was only 35 seconds behind the leader when they landed at Salt Lake City. A newspaper clipping stated when the race was over:

MENDELL CAPTURES RACE FROM OAKLAND

"Three crack racers, who roared across the finish line seconds apart to end the grueling 2200 mile dash from Oakland, were guests of honor today at the National Air Show at Cleveland.

"Loren Mendell of Culver City, former holder of the world endurance flight record, was the winner of the thrilling race that started from Oakland airport Sunday morning.

"W.J. (Joe) Barrows, Oakland forest patrol flier, was second, and Captain J.O. Donaldson of Newark, N.J., winner of the first trans-continental air race in 1919, was third....

"Barrows, a last minute entry, carried two passengers in his plane."

Another clipping from the Fairchild magazine: "A Fairchild 71 figured in 2 interesting racing events. Joe Barrows, a pilot who is affiliated with a Pacific Coast subsidiary of Fairchild, was prevailed upon to enter the Oakland derby just 2 hours before the take-off. He was not prepared for racing and had a heavy load, including passengers, built-in landing lights, and moving picture apparatus. As the race progressed some of the entries dropped out, leaving just three competitors. On some laps one would lead and on some another. On the last stage of the trip Barrows detoured to take some pictures of what he believed to be the Graf Zeppelin (it turned out to be the Los Angeles). When he arrived at Cleveland he was astonished to find that he was just 3 minutes behind the leader. He was awarded $1500.

The next day he entered the All Ohio race. As before, several contestants dropped out and by a strange coincidence the same 3 were left. Again he came in second with the other two in reversed positions. As a result of his casual entry in the derby he cleaned up a tidy sum."

Of course the 'tidy sum' went into the company's coffers. But Joe did get a windfall in an advertising letter to an oil company recommending the oil he had used. They sent him a check for $750. I hoped we could make a down payment on a house, but he was beginning to think of moving again. So the money paid up a few debts and bought a baby grand piano. (I could have used a washing machine.)

My brother Frank still lived with us when he wasn't out on aerial photography jobs. He was married that fall in Oregon. He had been on a mapping flight and brought his bride south in his plane.

"You're having an airplane honeymoon just as Joe and I did five years ago this month," I told him.

"I hope it won't be just like yours!" Frank answered fervently.

It wasn't. They took off at Roseburg and landed at Mills Field without any excitement, not even one forced landing on the way. To me it was very prosaic but some Roseburg versifier considered it romantic and published a bit of doggerel in the paper which read in part:

Young Lochinvar flew in from the south
And loving words were in his mouth.
Before we had a chance to turn
He gathered up our charming Ferne.
He bound her with a parachute,
And took again the southern route.

On our fifth wedding anniversary we flew up to Yreka and spent a few days with friends at a hunting lodge on the Klamath River. For the first time since I left Oregon I went into the hills hunting, cooked over a campfire and enjoyed the woods. Life on a city lot was not really to my liking. But years slipped by so fast and the children were small, and we hadn't been able to afford help. When Joe was away I lived in a world of bedtime stories, mashed vegetables and small children. We moved so often I had little social life and hadn't made many friends.

Just after New Years, 1930, we all flew to Portland where Joe went north on a mapping trip. We landed at the Portland Airport which was then on Swan Island in the Willamette River. I stayed with my married sister, Myrtle, while Joe mapped—rather, while he waited for mapping weather. It began to snow soon after we arrived. Margie Lou saw the snow piled on the window sill.

"Oh, Mommy, look at the white rain!" she exclaimed.

When the weather didn't clear we rented a furnished apartment by the week. The snow grew deeper. The Columbia River froze over and a car was driven across on the ice somewhere near the Interstate bridge.

The mapping finally over, we flew to Seattle to spend the night and to meet a pilot, Alex Holden, who was then connected with an aviation company flying between Seattle and Southeastern Alaska. This was my first view of the Puget Sound country and as I saw the sun setting behind the islands I fell in love with this beautiful region and thought then—and still think—that it is the loveliest corner of the whole United States.

During the spring and summer of 1930 Joe was on Forest Patrol work, or flying up and down the coast as far as British Columbia. He and his partner, Mr. Lowe, decided to work with Alex Holden and start a triangular air service from Seattle to Victoria and Vancouver. To incorporate or operate in Canada they had to make their headquarters there, and they chose the little English city of Victoria as a base. The flights would be made in planes equipped with pontoon floats, and for a terminal they wanted landing rights to the Inner Harbor. The Canadian Pacific Railroad attempted to block granting of permission for planes to land there.

During this period we met Frank Dorbrandt, one of Alaska's colorful bush pilots who had been with Carl Ben Eielson on flights into Siberia for furs. Eielson had been killed the previous winter on one of these flights. I remember one evening in Mr. Lowe's apartment high above San Francisco's lights when we sat spellbound listening to Frank tell about Alaska and his flying there. The very name, Alaska, spelled romance and adventure in far places.

We decided to move up to Victoria, but Joe had to make another trip East to take delivery of an airplane, a round-bodied, swift-flying Fleetster. He told me to move while he was gone, so I had the furniture crated and shipped ahead. My sister-in-law, Marjorie, and her daughter Jean drove north with me.

When the ferry docked the Empress Hotel and the Parliment Building grounds shone with lights. Our first view of Victoria was the most impressive I have ever had of a strange city. Usually one approaches through docks or railroad yards or industrial sections.

The imposing Empress Hotel looked much too grand and expensive for us, with three young children whose table manners were questionable, so we looked for a smaller place and found a residential hotel where we spent two nights. It was apparently inhabited by elderly spinsters, and they all looked at the children as if they were strange forms of animal life.

After a desperate search I found a furnished house we could rent for two weeks and we moved in thankfully. How blessed it is today to find motels with kitchen facilities almost everywhere, and what a boon for mothers with little folks.

While Marjorie herded children I house hunted in earnest. Out on Ten Mile Point, beyond Cadboro Bay, I found a new house situated on a lot which sloped down to the Sound. There was a magnificent view of the Olympic Mountains across the Straits and every ship entering the harbor steamed directly before the plate glass windows. Nearby were woodlands where we could hike to our heart's content. I only waited for Joe's approval before signing a lease and moving in.

He flew across Canada in the new, swift plane and landed in Vancouver where he was met by the mayor of the city. The paper heralded the Fleetster as the first of an airline which was to link the three Sound cities in a speedy transportation system—which it never did. Then Joe came on to Victoria for a two-day visit with his family.

Margie Lou had been having ear trouble and the doctor said her tonsils and adenoids must come out. As soon as her daddy arrived we had the operation performed and I left her all night in the hospital, a tiny mite in pink flannel pajamas in a big hospital bed.

Joe approved the Cadboro Bay house before he took off the next morning for San Francisco, taking Marjorie and Jean with him and leaving me alone—a stranger in a strange land.

I had the furniture trucked out to the house and then went to the hospital for Margie Lou, wrapping her in a blanket as I took her into the cold, empty house. First I uncrated a chair in which to deposit her. Then, alone and unaided, I uncrated the rest of the furniture and moved in.

Before electricity could be turned on a pole must be installed, so it was four days before we had lights or hot water. It was longer than that before a telephone was installed. It took a week to get a load of coal and it was two weeks before the paper boy began to leave a newspaper.

The house was dark and cold. I burned packing boxes in the fireplace as I unpacked, and put Margie Lou close beside the fire. Never have I felt so utterly alone, or so homesick.

At last the electricity was turned on and I plugged in the radio. The first program I tuned in was one we had listened to every afternoon in California so we felt less isolated. We had a new electric radio and had taken the battery set up to Uncle Frank and Aunt Edith to enjoy on their Oregon farm.

My sister, Edith, decided to come to spend the winter with me while she attended business college and it was wonderful to have her there for company. We were two miles beyond the end of the street car line as I hadn't thought of schools when I rented the house. Our milkman, who had several children, offered her a ride in the morning. So she rode to college on the milk truck, with the children delivering milk along the way. Evenings she walked home, or we met her if it was raining.

Meanwhile Joe had gone east again. During these months he and Mr. Lowe were remembering Frank Dorbrandt's stories of Alaska and the money to be made there in aviation. A big country with big distances, with few highways and only one railroad which ran from Seward to Fairbanks. A country which cried for airplane transportation.

On a Forest Patrol flight—Dad Barrows second from left with Joe at right.

In the new traveling suit. Mary Moore Barrows, Washington, D. C. 1929

Visiting celebrity from the West Coast,
W. Joe Barrows, Washington, D. C. 1929

Swan Island Airport, Portland about 1928

STRAIGHT DOWN

HEADED HOME

A Fairchild cabin monoplane, which carries a "mapping load" of pilot, camera operator, cameras, parachutes and more than 1000 pounds of fuel to an altitude of 17,500 feet within an hour of the take-off.

Newspaper picture of mapping plane

Passengers to Portland, Margie Lou and Teddy

Brother, Frank Moore and Margie Lou, 1928

Joe and Margie Lou on Bay Farm Island. 1927

Half of the Pacific Coast Air Service Company planes on Oakland's embryo airport. 1928

Fleetster which went through the ice at Telegraph Creek, B. C. On Anchorage airport, 1931

Fleetster under the ice

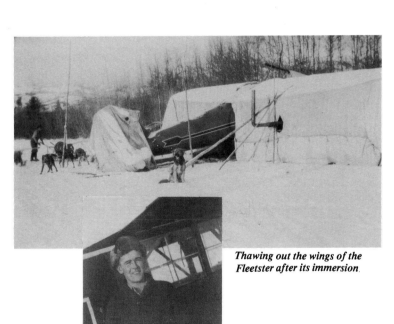

Thawing out the wings of the Fleetster after its immersion.

Everett Wasson, hero of the Burke search

Bob Martin and Emil Kading at their starvation camp

From left, Emil Kading, Bob Martin, Joe Walsh and Everett Wasson, just after they landed at Whitehorse

The proposed tri-city airline had struck a snag in Victoria, which was not then an air-minded city. The retired Englishmen who came there to spend their declining years didn't want their quiet shattered by the sound of airplane motors. They couldn't care less about fast transportation. Now, as I look back, I think they were probably right. Anyway, among the lovely gardens of Victoria lived people who had really learned to savor life's full goodness and richness.

Discouragement made Joe and Mr. Lowe decide that their Pacific International Airways should be really big and include Alaska as well as Canada and Puget Sound.

Alaskan mail contracts were coming up for bid, contracts which formerly had been carried by men driving dog teams. It was decided that we should bid on these contracts. Joe wrote from somewhere back east that he and the Lowes were flying to Alaska and asked me to go along. Six years before, when he had proposed to me, we had talked about flying to Alaska and I had even sent a letter of application for a teaching position in Anchorage. Now, at last, I was going to have a chance to go north.

I found a delightful English woman, a near neighbor, who would move into the house while I was gone to stay with Edith and the children. I will always have fond memories of her because she introduced the children, and me, to A.A. Milne's delightful "Winnie the Pooh" books.

Joe came to get me and we flew first to Seattle. Here an editor of the Seattle Times asked me to send in a report if we got any news about Captain E.J.A. Burke, who had been flying a pontoon-equipped Junkers with two passengers when he disappeared somewhere in the Yukon. Several planes were searching for him. One, piloted by Pat Renahan, had crashed somewhere near Ketchikan and more searchers were now looking for Renahan.

In the late afternoon we flew up over the Sound's lovely islands to Vancouver.

CHAPTER SIX

Man Hunt in the Yukon

Bell boys looked askance at masses of luggage piled in the lobby of the staid old Vancouver Hotel. There were duffel bags stuffed with woolen underwear and socks, boxes of food, axes, guns, fishing tackle—anything and everything which enterprising shopkeepers had said might be needed in 'outfitting' for the North.

This accumulation was all loaded into taxis and we drove to the airport in a slanting rain. I was filled with happiness. At last I was going to Alaska, and flying there as Joe and I had planned several years before.

Plans for the establishment of a tri-city air service were abandoned, at least temporarily, as the powerful Canadian Pacific Railroad Company continued to block a lease on the landing base they wanted in Victoria's inner harbor. Joe and Mr. Lowe had decided to enlarge the scope of the Pacific International Airways to include Alaska. Now, in the late fall of 1930, we were going north to bid on mail contracts.

Joe's wealthy partners, Mr. and Mrs. Lowe, were going along. They had also invited a friend, Miss Jean Boyd to come along for the ride. We were all anticipating a delightful trip into the romantic North.

Two planes were waiting at the airport. Joe was flying the trim-bodied Fleetster he had brought out from the East. Harry Blunt was flying a Fairchild. Harry had learned to fly with Joe and had worked into the Forest Patrol business with him in California.

The planes were loaded, and loaded—and then still more duffel bags were packed in. Included in the baggage were two awkward-shaped pairs of skis to be mounted on the planes as soon as we reached snow. And there were six people and their rations who must someway crowd into the planes.

It was found that the planes just couldn't take off with this overload, so there on the muddy runways the baggage was hastily repacked and several things were discarded.

At last it seemed that Jean Boyd and I were part of the excess baggage. Almost before we realized what was happening, the planes were disappearing into the North, leaving us on the runway amidst a pile of gear.

"Meet us at Whitehorse," the departing adventurers had shouted.

At the Canadian Pacific Steamship offices we found that a ship left for Skagway every two weeks in the winter.

"Can we get a train from there to Whitehorse?" we asked.

"I don't know," answered the agent. "Sometimes it runs and sometimes it doesn't. The track might be blocked with snow and then you'd have to go by dog team. It's a gamble."

This was my first experience with the colossal ignorance about the North I often found even in Vancouver and Seattle—gateway cities.

We decided to gamble and boarded a tiny Canadian Pacific steamer, the "Princess Norah", which was to take us to Skagway.

The trip up the Inside Passage is delightful, between wooded islands and steeply rising mountains where waterfalls tumble over crags and snow caps the peaks. At Alert Bay we saw our first totem poles in front of weathered cabins where Indian families lived. It was snowing in Ketchikan so we didn't do much sightseeing. Again at Juneau we tramped on snowy streets, the soft crunch of snow delightful to Californians.

A telegram from Joe was delivered here. The planes were held in interior British Columbia with bad weather. Snow had fallen and the skis were mounted, but the next morning a chinook wind swept the ground bare so they were changed back to wheels. It looked as if we would reach the Yukon ahead of the others after all.

On a windy, blustery morning we steamed up Lynn Canal and docked at Skagway. The rocky cliffs above the pier were covered with paintings, insignia of boats and a huge painted skull of Soapy Smith—the bandit who had terrorized Skagway in the early days of the gold rush.

The captain hurried the unloading so that he could be out of the canal in daylight as there were icebergs floating in the water.

Jean and I registered at the Golden North Hotel, built before plumbing (which had been added later) and operated by Mrs. Dedman, a resident of Skagway since the days of the gold rush. Darkness fell early. We looked out of our corner windows upon a street teeming with memories of hordes of gold seekers, of open saloons and dance halls. All we saw was a woman hurrying home with a bag of groceries and a lone Malemute pattering along the snowy street. Most of the buildings were boarded up, empty and deserted.

While we waited for the train we visited the Pullen House and Mrs. Pullen in a Princess gown of the style of '98, her magnificent hair coiled around her shapely head, showed us her museum and told us of her personal experiences in the gold rush.

51

The White Pass & Yukon, a narrow-gauge train, took us to Whitehorse. It crawled along the edges of cliffs and crossed gulches on spidery bridges. Yet this railroad paid for itself in its first year of operation.

It was dark when we arrived at Whitehorse, but most of the town's population turned out to meet the train.

A tall, handsome young man stepped up to me and spoke my name. I looked up in astonishment.

"I'm Everett Wasson," he introduced himself. "I learned to fly in Oakland with your brother Frank, and I'm flying for the Treadwell-Yukon Company in the same plane your husband sold them—the one he brought from New York to Seattle."

The world isn't so large!

Everett was in Whitehorse to aid in the search for Captain Burke. With him was his French-Canadian mechanic, Emil Forrest, and a prospector, Joe Walsh, who knew the Yukon. Bad weather was holding them grounded.

The Whitehorse Inn was just a block up the snowy street. A huge stove in the cheerful lobby gave out inviting warmth, and we had a delicious meal in the adjoining restaurant.

In the following days we hiked to Whitehorse Rapids and on to Miles Canyon, dreaded obstacles to boatmen who ran the Yukon on the way to the Klondike. We saw the cabin where Robert Service had lived while he worked in a local bank, and the cabin of Sam McGee. I hadn't known that Sam McGee was a real person! Every day we called at the telegraph office to watch the operator 'work' his telegraph line. The operator informed us that Joe had reached Telegraph Creek, on the Stikine River, and found out what the weather was like, and what Joe's plans were for the day.

When the weather looked good we got up and breakfasted with Everett, Emil, and Joe Walsh while it was still dark—daylight didn't come until nine o'clock. Then we rode up to the airport—on a plateau above the town and the Yukon River—seated on a sled drawn by a tractor. Gasoline cans were piled around us. Joe Walsh carried his box of grub and a bag of chocolate bars which were good will offerings to any Indians they saw.

Day dawned as we reached the field. A fire was started in the hangar stove and cans of oil set on to heat. A heater was put under the plane's motor and while the oil and motor warmed up the men loaded the plane, sharpened their axes, swept snow from the wings and fuselage, and did other chores.

As regular equipment the plane carried two heavy eider-down sleeping bags, a Yukon stove, cans for draining the oil, five or six extra cases of gas, a box of food containing staples such as rice, flour, dry beans, coffee and sugar. There were three pairs of snow shoes in the baggage compartment. During the search Everett and Joe Walsh tramped more than two hundred miles on them—all of it through unbroken, waist-deep snow.

Captain Burke had left Atlin, a mining camp in northern British Columbia, on October 10th, flying to Liard Post with his mechanic, Emil Kading—a young man just four years from Germany—and a prospector who had chartered the plane.

After they were gone a week an alarm went out. It was known that they had left their food and snowshoes in Atlin to make room for sluice boxes in the plane, and in the Yukon there were no corner groceries. At that time less than five thousand people lived in an area twice the size of California, and most of them were along the Yukon River.

Day after day Everett took off on his search. In all he made eleven flights into the Liard region, none less than 200 miles round trip. Today this area is crossed by the Alcan Highway but then there was no settlement to the east, with the exception of two or three isolated trading posts and a few scattered Indian camps. Gas had to be carried for the round trip, also food and ammunition.

"Don't worry about us," Joe Walsh often said. "With what we have in the plane we could stay out all winter."

I was surprised that Everett carried no maps with him.

"The existing maps are hopeless," he grinned. "That country has never been surveyed. Look at a large map of the Yukon Territory and you'll see that many mountain ranges, and most of the eastern rivers, are just dotted in. The map maker had only a general idea. The watershed of the Jennings River is entirely different from what is marked on the map. The Liard curves around almost to Wolf Lake, and Wolf Lake isn't where it is marked. There are hundreds of lakes not on the map at all. If I tried to fly by a map—after I've been over the region—I'd get lost. A pilot here learns to study landmarks, to learn the country. The Indians don't get lost, but most white men have no sense of direction."

When they began their search the lakes weren't frozen solid. In one landing the tail skid dug through the thin ice. Everett hastily "gave her the gun" and pulled to shore. Many lakes were too small to land on. Once they chopped down trees for half a mile ahead to make a runway. They snowshoed tracks in the soft, sticky snow, tramping the path down hard and allowing it to freeze overnight to help a take-off. Indians at the camps where they stopped to inquire helped in cutting wood and snowshoeing runways.

The telegraph operator gave us disastrous news. Down in Telegraph Creek Harry Blunt had crashed the Fairchild in an attempted take-off. Both his legs were smashed when the motor folded back on them. Joe started to taxi across the ice of the little lake on which they had landed, rushing to Harry's rescue, and the Fleetster dropped through a weak spot in the ice. Joe went under the icy water, escaping through a trap door in the top of the cockpit. Both Harry and Joe were in the little infirmary at Telegraph Creek, with only a veterinarian in attendance. One plane was a complete wash-out, and the other was in the lake, its wings resting on the top of the ice. Joe had inflammatory rheumatism and was unable to walk or to use his right hand even to feed himself. Harry had two broken legs.

There was nothing I could do but wait.

Jean's vacation ended and she returned to 'the states'. I walked, and read, and made friends in the town, and waited.

Down in Telegraph Creek Joe knew that Harry must be brought to the hospital and so he must salvage the plane which was under the ice. He got a dog team to take him on a sled to the lake where, lying on his side in the sled, he directed the salvage work. A lane was chopped through the ice and the plane was towed to the shore. Tents were put over the wings and fires were lighted under them. The inside of the wings were solid blocks of ice, as was the inside of the cabin. The entire motor had to be serviced, every cylinder checked. All the instruments were ruined. It seemed impossible that the Fleetster would ever fly again.

Meanwhile Everett carried on the Burke search single-handed. On one trip he planned to go to the Lower Liard trading post to inquire what Burke's plans had been. We gathered magazines to send to the isolated trader. However, in landing at an Indian camp thirty miles up river they learned that Burke had passed over, heading north. So they camped there for the night and left the magazines with an Indian who had been 'outside' to school.

"All the Indians squatted on the floor," Joe Walsh told me. "The chief had a woman's magazine you put in. 'What's the matter with white squaw?' he asked, seeing pictures of thin fashion models. 'No grub outside? White squaw too thin. Better come in here. Plenty caribou, moose, here.' "

"The cabin was clean, too," Everett commented. "The woman even washed her hands before cooking breakfast. And one woman had a black velvet dress. She must have put it on in our honor. It had a few spots and pitch stains on it, but it was real velvet."

A hundred miles north of Liard Post they found a trapper with his Indian wife and two, blue-eyed children. Hospitably, the trapper urged them to stay overnight and forced them to occupy the cabin while the owners moved out into a brush 'wickie'. Here their dinner consisted of moose nose 'with the fur on'. The trapper, eager for companionship, mushed to the plane with them the next morning.

"Squaws are good women for the north," he commented. "Only one trouble with them—they're all lousy."

Following the winding river, Everett started back to Whitehorse. In a curve, east of Wolf Lake, he saw the Junkers plane frozen in the ice below.

"It seemed too good to be true, sitting there apparently unharmed. I could see the wing's shadow on the snow, so I knew they made a good landing. There were no tracks in the snow around the plane."

The next trip they landed on the nearest lake and mushed over, hoping to find traces of the men. The plane was apparently undamaged, but there was no sign of its occupants. Joe searched the banks, where the men had evidently camped for some days, and found a blazed tree with a message scratched with a knife blade.

"October 17. Leaving for Wolf Lake. Grub supply low.
Paddy. Bob. Emil."

They had never reached Wolf Lake. And why had they started upstream, when down river there were Indian camps within thirty miles?

There was only one chance left. Across the Pelly Mountains was an isolated trading post, Pelly Banks. Perhaps the lost men had stumbled onto trap lines of Indians from beyond the ridge, and had been taken to this post. Everett and Joe set out on what was to be their last flight, to Pelly Banks. A Mounted Policeman, with dog team, was in readiness if this trip also proved a failure. Everett planned to take him to the plane and let him follow the trail from the ground.

But on this flight, while circling for a pass through the mountains, Everett saw a fire. It flared up suddenly, a typical signal fire. Everett circled low over the fire and saw two men on the ground waving their arms. Joe Walsh opened the rear door of the plane and kicked out two boxes of food. One of them almost hit Emil Kading on the head.

Everett landed on the nearest lake, about ten miles away. Taking the three pairs of snowshoes, their sleeping bags, and a piece of dried moosemeat, they started hiking. Darkness fell about three o'clock in December and with darkness the two starving men, conserving their strength and their firewood, had crawled into their sleeping bags. The airmen missed the pitiful camp and mushed on in the darkness. At midnight they concluded that they had somehow gone too far so they 'siwashed' in their sleeping bags until daylight, with only dried meat to eat after a long hike in

55

waist-deep snow.

At dawn, Everett checked landmarks and turned back. It was again dark when they found the men. They shouted at intervals to attract their attention. Emil Kading heard the shout, and, too weak to answer, fired his last bullet.

The two ragged, bearded, emaciated men were found in a trampled place in the snow, no shelter but the gray sky above them, nothing around them but their sleeping bags, a five gallon gas can, the empty gun, and a blunted axe.

"Any boy scout could have done better," Joe Walsh commented later.

Captain Burke was dead, of starvation. The living were Emil Kading, mechanic, and Bob Martin, prospector.

That night Joe Walsh cooked a dinner of mush and rice which could be easily digested by long idle stomachs.

"Joe Walsh makes the best coffee I ever tasted," Mr. Martin said later. "But we hadn't had any for over two months. We boiled what tea we had for two weeks and then smoked up the leaves when we ran out of tobacco."

In spite of their caution Mr. Martin had stomach cramps after eating.

The next morning they went to the plane. Mr. Martin wore the extra pair of snowshoes, and Emil Kading wore make-shift skis whittled out of a spruce log. Everett broke trail.

"I tried to keep up with that big moose," Mr. Martin said. "But he took steps two yards apart, and he doesn't know what it means to be tired."

Everett Wasson was six feet two and weighed around two hundred pounds. Tramping through the snow for two months had made him in good condition.

When Emil Kading reached the Fairchild he was staggering, as weak as a baby. He had strained his heart cutting wood, hunting, caring for the others while he had been slowly starving to death.

They camped beside the plane and that night the mercury dropped to thirty below zero. The previous week it had been almost at thawing. The starving men had been rescued just in time as their lowered vitality wouldn't have brought them through the cold.

Joe Walsh put up the tent, built a cozy fire in the Yukon stove, and cooked a big pot of rice. The next day he added powdered eggs to the diet he had prescribed.

It had been the tenth of October when Captain "Paddy" Burke had left Atlin. Now, two months later, on the tenth of December, Emil Forrest and I went up to the airport with the tractor and the big sled. It was a perfect flying day and we expected the Fairchild in. We built a roaring fire in the hangar.

At just twelve o'clock we heard an airplane motor and saw the red Fairchild circling to land. As it came in we saw that there were more than two men in the cabin. Excitedly we hurried to lay poles for the skis to taxi on, so they would not freeze to the snow. Joe Walsh climbed out.

"We have Kading and Martin here," he said. "Burke is dead."

There were only four or five telephones in Whitehorse and one was in the hangar. With all the instincts of a true reporter, I tore to it, cranked the number of the telegraph operator and breathlessly gave him a wire to the Seattle Times.

The operator sent it just as the clock struck twelve. Then he closed the office and went home to lunch. No one else could send out news until the office opened at one o'clock. I found out later that the Seattle Times scooped all other papers by over an hour. And it was a real scoop!

Hanging up the telephone receiver, I ran back to see two bearded, ragged men climb slowly from the plane. Bob Martin with heavy gray beard and iron gray hair, looking old and broken. Emil Kading with thin, worn face, heavy dark beard, and long hair curling to his shoulders. There were hollows under his eyes and shrunken skin tight over his cheek bones. The men shivered in the cold and came gladly into the hangar. When they were warmed Mr. Martin saw the scales upon which the Mayo freight was weighed.

"I've lost sixty-five pounds," he announced. Emil Kading had lost twenty.

"Poor Paddy," they sighed. "He had no reserve. He wasn't well when we left Atlin."

"Only an hour and a half from their camp to Whitehorse," Everett commented. An hour and a half from death—from starvation!

I kept looking at the men; both were dirty and ragged with unkempt hair and beards. Their eyes were deep sunken, glassy and staring.

We sat on empty boxes by the fire while the airmen took care of the plane. The rescued men began to talk, half hesitatingly and yet half eagerly, as if in telling they could forget the hardships they had suffered.

"Why did you land?" I asked.

"We landed first in a snowstorm," Kading said, slurring his 'd's and 'th's in a German accent. "Then the next day we took off again and flew about seven minutes before a blinding snowstorm forced us down again. The weather changes over there every time you wink your eye. We knocked a hole in the pontoon, not bad, but it filled with water. We stayed at the plane seven days and no one came for us so we started walking. The river was running fast so we couldn't fix the pontoon.''

"Why didn't you build a raft and float down river?'' Joe Walsh asked practically. "There was an Indian camp just thirty miles below where you landed.''

"We didn't see it in the snowstorm,'' Martin answered, and then added, "I had a hunch to go up river.''

This hunch turned out tragically.

"Burke was already so weak we only walked three or four miles a day,'' Kading went on. "Our camps were pretty close together. We had a cache about thirty miles from where they found us. We were trying to reach it.''

In the North a 'cache' is a place where food is stored.

We wondered why this strong young man hadn't walked in. The summer before he had walked seventy miles to Atlin in record time, after a forced landing.

"I couldn't leave the others,'' he said quietly. "There was only one axe and one gun. They were older. I had to hunt and cut wood for them.'' He had almost given his life for the others.

Mr. Martin froze his toes and was unable to walk farther. Burke was succumbing to kidney trouble, added to the slow starvation.

Every day Kading hunted, tramping through the soft snow, heartbreaking work without snowshoes. But there was no game in the country. The moose and caribou were farther up along the timber line.

"In twenty-three days we had a duck and four squirrels,'' Kading continued. "We had only eleven bullets when we left the plane. I had to hit whatever I shot at, and I had to 'crease' the squirrels or there wouldn't be anything left of them.''

Four squirrels and a duck in twenty-three days, divided between three hungry men.

"One day I saw a moose.'' A moose with its rich red meat would have meant salvation. "But he was too far away and I was excited. I missed him.'' In his flat tone you sensed the tragedy.

"And one night,'' Martin interjected. "Just before Paddy died, two wolves came into camp, so close we could have hit them with rocks. Big brutes they were, too. They hung around for quite a while, but our shouts and the fire drove them away. We were afraid.''

"On the eighth of November,'' Kading went on, "Burke wrote a letter to his wife. I have it here.'' He pulled out a folded piece of dirty paper, a bill form. "And he had a ring he wanted to give to his wife. But his hand got so thin the ring fell off and we couldn't find it until after he died. On the fifteenth, when I shot the caribou, he said he was going to be all right again and not to bother with the ring. I found it when I scraped the snow away from a log where he had been sitting."

The caribou wandered into their camp in the night and they saw it next morning. Burke prayed while Kading aimed, and the shot went true. They boiled meat in their five gallon gas can and Burke drank two or three cups of broth, but there isn't as much nourishment in caribou as there is in moose meat. They cut the liver in little bits and roasted it on the ends of willow sticks. Burke ate some. That was the last day he walked.

"He took a few steps that day. The next day Bob and I held him and helped him around but he was numb already in the feet and legs. We couldn't do anything for him. It was awful to sit there and see him getting weaker and to know our turn was coming next. Paddy didn't have the reserve we did. He went first."

"He died in my arms on the twentieth of November." Martin choked up then. Neither of them could talk calmly about 'Paddy'. It was evident that they had loved him. "We made a log cache and buried him in it. Then we went on a few miles. We couldn't stand staying there by it."

Kading's splended strength was beginning to fail. He no longer hunted but conserved his energy to cut firewood. They went to bed at three o'clock when the sun went down, pulling their sleeping bags close together for warmth—"just the blue sky over us."

Everett and Joe Walsh found the Junkers frozen in the Liard just the day after Burke died. The two starving men had seen the plane fly over.

"I had been out in the woods," Kading said. "We had no fire going. It was the saddest day of my life when I saw that plane go out of sight without finding us."

A few days later they again saw it go over and disappear. This time Emil Kading had firewood cut to make a signal fire, but he got it started too late and the plane went on across the hills.

"I pulled the wood off quick," he said wearily. "I couldn't cut more."

Tears filled my eyes as I pictured them, their hopes ebbing with their strength, as they saw the red monoplane growing smaller in the west.

Saturday all the meat left was on one leg bone, from the knee to the hoof, just a few bites apiece. There was only one more bullet. The end was in sight. It was growing colder after the warm spell of the previous week, the warmth which had saved their lives.

That afternoon the plane returned. Kading heard it coming and instantly pushed the wood on the fire. From the airplane Everett saw the smoke.

Whitehorse's entire population turned out to meet the rescued and the rescuers—the twenty-three-year-old California aviator and Joe Walsh, the prospector who had proved his knowledge of the Yukon.

In the restaurant I sat across from Mr. Martin and I saw his emotion. He bowed his head in his hands.

"If we only had Paddy here the party would be complete," he said.

Often their talk turned to Mrs. Burke and her two children. I pitied her; I was an aviator's wife, too.

After lunch Martin and Kading went to have baths and then visited the barber. About four o'clock I was talking to Joe Walsh in the hotel lobby when a young man came in and sat down beside us. He was dressed neatly in a suit and I looked at him curiously, wondering who he was. Suddenly it dawned on me that this was Emil Kading, twenty years younger with the removal of the wild beard.

"I take the old clothes by the ends of my fingers and chuck them in the furnace," he said. "They are gone and forgotten."

Rolling up his pants leg he pointed to dark spots on the skin along the shin bone. "I thought it was dirt, but when I scrubbed it would not come off."

"Scurvy," Joe Walsh pronounced. "You got in just in time."

The ominous word recalled that Burke's plane had been found only three miles from the mouth of Scurvy Creek where many years earlier another gold-seeking party had lost their lives.

Forty-eight hours after they came in they were different men. Kading went with the rest of us to a dancing party.

"I von't dance," he said. "I'm still too veak."

But when a Mountie played the first chords on the piano he got up and bowed to me. As I fox-trotted with him he grinned,

"A few nights ago I was sitting out there in the Liard waiting to die. But I'm better dan ten dead men yet."

The Dominion government awarded Everett Wasson fifteen hundred dollars, and Joe Walsh five hundred, in appreciation of their heroic rescue flights.

Everett made a last trip to the Liard to bring out Burke's body, accompanied by a Sergeant of the Royal Canadian Mounted Police.

As we started to the field to meet Everett we heard an airplane roar over town. It wasn't the Fairchild's motor. I looked skyward to see the dark blue, bullet-like body of the Fleetster banking overhead, and I reached it as it stopped taxiing.

Inside was Harry Blunt, blanket-wrapped, lying on the cabin floor. Joe was in the cockpit, a cockpit without instruments. He had flown up from Telegraph Creek by sight and by ear. Beside him was Joe Morrison, an old army mechanic who lived in Telegraph Creek, and who had helped him salvage the plane.

I gasped as they lifted Harry Blunt from the cabin and laid him gently on the sled. Then I gasped again as they climbed back into the plane and lifted Joe out. He was unable to walk, unable to use his right hand, and yet he had just flown three hundred miles over totally uninhabited, mountainous country. Joe Morrison had worked the stabilizer and managed the mechanical part of the flying.

It was Joe Morrison who told me how my husband had been carried to the Fleetster day after day, how he had lain on his side in the cabin to work with his left hand to repair the plane and get it ready to bring Harry to the hospital.

Captain Burke's stiffly frozen body rode to town with us on the same sled.

I attended the inquest and heard the jurors give a verdict of "death by exposure and starvation." They recommended that planes flying in the north be equipped, during the winter, with axe, gun, fifty rounds of ammunition, snowshoes, a sleeping bag for each passenger, and food for thirty days. Each pilot should have a rudimentary knowledge of woodcraft.

The Arctic is a country in which nature and the elements are mighty forces, never to be forgotten.

Everett flew Captain Burke's body to Atlin for burial.

It was the nineteenth of December when Joe arrived in Whitehorse. The doctor ordered him to bed. But Christmas day he got up and walked with me, under the shimmering swirl of the northern lights at thirty below zero, to the home of the Northern Commercial store manager. Here we had a delicious dinner of turkey, cranberry sauce, sweet potatoes, mince pie, and all the trimmings.

CHAPTER SEVEN

Introduction to Alaska

New Year's Day, 1931, at a hotel in Whitehorse, Yukon Territory. Joe was still in bed, crippled with rheumatism. But a day or two later he flew back to Telegraph Creek with food supplies for the people there, and brought Mr. and Mrs. Lowe up to Whitehorse. Although Joe needed to go to a hospital, he felt that he must continue the trip. The Fleetster was not really airworthy after its immersion in an icy lake, but there were shops and mechanics in Fairbanks.

It was decided that I should go back to Victoria to the children. I had already been away from them two months, leaving Edith with them for a lonely Christmas far away from any of the family. I climbed aboard the White Pass & Yukon train bound for Skagway. Everett Wasson was on the same train with his fiancee, a nurse from the Whitehorse Hospital. They were to be married in Vancouver and planned a honeymoon trip back to New York to the Fairchild factory.

And Joe flew on to Alaska. Letters were postmarked from different places—Fairbanks, Anchorage, Nulato, Nome, Seward. Our company had been successful bidders on the star route mail contracts in competition with dog teams, and Joe had to survey the proposed routes. In a Seward Hospital he lost his appendix, his tonsils, and a broken toe—all under the same anesthetic. Ten days after the appendectomy Frank Dorbrandt flew him to Anchorage, and he was in the air again. On a trip down the Yukon he was grounded at Nulato with the flu and a kindly priest put him to bed at the mission there. I got these disturbing bulletins fifteen-hundred miles away.

In the meantime we enjoyed springtime in Victoria. Edith continued with her business college course, and Margie Lou was enrolled in a small neighborhood kindergarten.

It was April before Joe came south again, and he was so gaunt and haggard that Teddy didn't recognize him when he came down the gangplank. The child had seen his daddy only once in nearly a year, and now Joe weighed just 128 pounds and his clothes hung loosely on his six foot frame.

We took a hurried trip to California where Joe went to a hospital for a rest and check-up, and where Edith enrolled in an Oakland business college to complete her course. Then I went back to

Victoria with the children and Joe sailed northward to Seward and interior Alaska.

On a Sunday morning in June, just a few weeks later, I received a telegram from Anchorage.

"Catch the next boat north."

Alaska Steamship sailings were on Saturday from Seattle. By Thursday afternoon I had washed and ironed the curtains, arranged for all of the furniture in a seven-room house to be crated and shipped, and was ready to catch the ferry. In Seattle on Friday I took the car to the docks and checked on our reservations for passage.

We spent the afternoon at Woodland Park visiting the zoo. A Kodiak bear, standing almost as tall as a horse, was in one cage, with an inscription reading, "Caught in the vicinity of Cook Inlet, Alaska." We knew that Anchorage was on Cook Inlet.

"Mommy, I don't want to go to Alaska," my four-year-old son caught my hand and peered up fearfully at the huge bear. "Not if there are bears like that one around."

Next morning when the S.S. Aleutian steamed out into Puget Sound northward bound, we were aboard. This time we were not tourists, as I had been on the Princess Norah to Skagway; we were going north to stay. We were to be Alaskans.

A steamer voyage is recommended as a rest cure, but traveling with two lively children is not restful. I spent hours reading aloud from our new "Winnie the Pooh" books, trying to quiet my two wiggly children, or I stood with a hand firmly on the collar of each one to keep them from falling overboard. They wanted to see everything, and I guess they did.

One afternoon I stood at the rail during one of the few periods when they were both napping at once and heard a young man next to me complaining to another passenger,

"I sure don't get much sleep. There's some aviator's wife in the stateroom next to mine with two small children and they are awake by four every morning."

I sympathized with him silently, not letting him know who I was. They woke me up, too.

Leaving Juneau, the ship turned west and just as we entered the Gulf of Alaska Teddy saw an iceberg floating past.

"Oh, here's the frozen northland!" he cried.

The Gulf crossing wasn't very rough but we spent most of our time in our bunks, Margie Lou in the top one, and Teddy and I in the lower. None of us were good sailors. Beyond Cape St. Elias we were back in sheltered water.

Although this wasn't quite far enough north to be 'the land of the midnight sun' we had wonderful long sunsets. I stayed up most of the night watching the changing colors of the sky and sea. The water turned into shades of pink and lavendar and wine; the sky was filled with crimson and gold clouds lasting hour after hour until sunrise colors mingled with those of the sunset. There was no darkness, just the twilight tinged with color.

At Cordova, Joe surprised us by getting on the ship to ride the rest of the journey to Seward with us. The next's day's scenery was magnificent. Giant peaks rose sheer from the water's edge. There were smooth reaches where reflections were mirrored. Waterfalls tumbled down precipitous slopes. Little canneries were tucked in tiny coves. We steamed up to Columbia Glacier and the boat's whistle was blown in the hope that reverberations would cause icebergs to break off. Across the glacier's face were incredible streaks of blue, a pale blue in places with bands of deeper indigo. The huge river of ice towered high above the ship. Now and then a piece broke off with a powdery shower of spray and plunged into the water with a resounding splash, to turn over a time or two and emerge as a baby iceberg.

At Valdez our car was put ashore, to be driven over the highway to Fairbanks, where Joe said we would probably be stationed. Mosquitoes swarmed thickly and we slapped and swatted. Behind the little town loomed a huge dead glacier, slowly receding. Joe pointed to second-story windows of the old buildings to show how deep the snow had been during the previous winter. The old buildings, the mosquitoes, the tales of hard winters, the forbidding glacier, all depressed me so that I went back to the ship's cabin and cried. At that moment I would have gladly returned on the south-bound trip of the S.S. Aleutian.

Next morning when we docked at Seward and I saw beautiful Resurrection Bay, with the mountains around it, when I went ashore and walked through the town past the clean little stores and met the friendly people, I forgot all about being homesick for 'the States'. Never again in Alaska was I homesick—from then on Alaska *was* home.

Alex Holden had flown down in a Fairchild equipped with pontoons, and he took us up to Anchorage. In all the years since I had been associated with aviation, this was the first time I had ridden with any pilot but Joe. Now my husband sat in the cabin with me and held Teddy on his knee.

Mountain sheep browsed on the hills close beside the wing tips as we sped northward through the passes and over the edge of Cook Inlet, dropping down to a landing on Lake Spenard, just outside of Anchorage.

"Hello, Mary," shouted Harry and Ida Blunt, "Welcome to Alaska."

64

How good it was to see old friends, and to hear my first name called after the year of formality of English Victoria! Immediately I felt among friends.

We drove to town along a pretty country road, through groves of birch trees, between clumps of flaming purple fireweed and tangles of wild roses to the wide streets of Anchorage, then a town of about 2500 population.

This was a railroad town, laid out during the construction of the Alaska Railroad and didn't—like most Alaskan mining towns—just grow. The streets were at right angles to one another, the buildings were moderately new and up to date and it might have been a progressive small town in Montana except that around it were the breath-taking hills, before it the waters of Cook Inlet, and to the north the snowy summit of Mt. McKinley.

The hotel lobby contained an impressive Sydney Laurence painting of Mount McKinley. We put our suitcases in assigned rooms, cleaned up, and then walked over to Blunt's little bungalow for dinner.

After the meal Joe and Harry went out to the Lake to see about the planes, and Ida and I washed the dishes and visited about all that had happened since we had left San Bruno. The children played outside in the sunny evening. Suddenly I looked at the clock and discovered in amazement that it was ten o'clock. The sun still rode high in the sky. Hastily I called the children and took them to the hotel to bed, amid protests that it wasn't even dark so it couldn't be bedtime. At midnight I took a snapshot from the hotel window, to prove that it was light.

The next day was the Fourth of July and the children had firecrackers, which their father enjoyed. In the afternoon we went to a baseball game. This was like the Fourths of my childhood, bringing memories of a little Colorado town. At the close of my first twenty-four hours in Anchorage, I was madly in love with the interior of Alaska and with the easy friendliness of the people.

There was a vacant apartment in the Shonbeck building and we rented it and moved in with our suitcases. Our furniture was to go on north to Fairbanks, so I had to be satisfied with "furnished rooms." The living room contained a pull-down bed, the kitchen had a three-burner kerosene stove and a dry-goods box nailed outside the window for a cooler. Beyond was a room with twin beds for the children. The rent was $62.50, which seemed exorbitant, but would be far less than staying in a hotel and eating in restaurants. I unpacked our clothes and started housekeeping, discovering in dismay that the prices of food were double what they were 'Outside'. Everything had to be shipped by steamer, and then brought to Anchorage over the railroad. "It's the freight rate," was the usual answer to any protest about high prices.

One of our pilots, Lon Cope, lived in the same apartment building with his attractive wife, Margaret, who soon became my best friend in Anchorage. Lon, with Alex Holden, Harry Blunt, and Al Monsen, were our piloting force. Harry's legs had recovered well from the crash of the winter before. Joe was manager of the company, and flew as many hours as any of the pilots. There was an office in the Hewitt Photo Shop Building, not far from the hotel, and a stenographer kept track of the business there. Two mechanics, Larry Davis and 'Jinks' Ames, completed the force of the PIA.

Two weeks after I reached Anchorage Joe asked me to go with him on a flight over the route of our proposed mail lines. Service on the Yukon and Kuskokwin was to begin the first of November. It was necessary to stop at each village to meet the people, to appoint agents, interview postmasters, select places for gasoline caches for the winter's flying supplies, and arrange to have the gasoline on the ground before the close of river boat navigation. Naturally I was enthusiastic about such an opportunity to see my new home territory.

Ida Blunt and her teen-age daughter, Maxine, offered to take care of the children so that I might go.

Lake Spenard was too small to allow the takeoff of a loaded plane, and as we had two passengers—an Anchorage attorney and his wife—Joe flew across to Cook Inlet. Here there are unusually high tides, almost as great as those in the Bay of Fundy. We were carried out of the plane across a sea of gray mud flats. I watched in fascination as the plane raced over the water, rose on the step, and became air-borne. I found flying from water exciting and very different from a wheel take-off on an airport.

Float planes were really opening up Alaska. There were very few real air fields upon which one could land with wheels. But there were everywhere water systems, lakes and rivers which all summer long from break-up of the ice in the spring until freeze-up in the fall were natural landing places. Then in the winter when ground and lakes and rivers were frozen solidly wheels and pontoons gave way to skis.

Pilots who had been accustomed to landing on packed runways had to learn new skills in landing and taking off on water. They must *read* the water, the current, the wind, the waves. They must know what to expect of their plane and how heavy a load the pontoons would lift. It wasn't just a question of running a little farther to get air speed; either the pontoons would get up on top of the waves, 'on the step', or they wouldn't. Anne Lindbergh devoted almost a whole book to telling of their experiences in trying to take off on floats from the west coast of Africa when the wind wasn't strong enough to provide good waves. "Listen, the Wind", is written by an aviator's wife who sat in the cockpit, saw the spray as the plane taxied through the water, and felt despair when it wouldn't rise.

Once in the air, the Alaska Railroad provided a track for us as we headed north. The Susitna River wound down from the Alaska Range. Soon we encountered rain and beyond Curry the mountains closed in on either side, "came pouring in the windows" as Al Monsen said once. Weather and visibility worsened and Joe circled Summit Lake, planning to land there if he couldn't get through the pass. Below was a narrow, rapid river, milk-colored from glacial deposits. Mount McKinley was hiding behind the clouds.

Through the pass and out into sunshine, a rainbow gleaming on the clouds. Ahead was the wide Tanana Valley, light blue in the foreground, deepening to cobalt where the flat earth and the sky met in the hazy distance. Leaving the railroad, we cut across to the muddy Tanana, flying over fish wheels which turned in the water, over racks of bright red salmon drying on the banks.

Fairbanks sprawled on both sides of Chena Slough, a town of pleasant homes, log cabins, unbelieveably bright flower beds, streets lined with silver-trunked birches. This was my first view of the city which is 'the golden heart of Alaska', the city which captured my heart. Then, of course, it was not really a city, as the population was about 2,500, or even less.

We dropped down to a landing on the slough about a mile from town. Elton and Bob Busby ferried us to shore in a row boat. Later Bob became one of Alaska's famous dog mushers. We climbed the green banks and were immediately attacked by hordes of hungry mosquitoes.

During our week in Fairbanks the sun shone almost twenty-four hours a day and the sunset skies were incredibly beautiful. I spent the week househunting and found a house for rent which would be available in October. It was occupied so that I could not go inside but we rented it, sight unseen, as houses were at a premium and this one had inside plumbing—something quite rare then.

There was an atmosphere about this friendly town which I liked. Anchorage might be a town in Montana or Idaho, but Fairbanks could be nowhere but in the interior of Alaska. The Northern Commercial Company store displayed skis and dog harness and mukluks and dehydrated potatoes in the windows. Jewelry stores featured nugget jewelry. The telephone central office asked for the name of the person you were calling instead of a number, and often told you where you might find the person.

"Mrs. Jones is visiting over at Mrs. Smith's house right now. Do you want me to try to reach her there?"

We went out to the University to see this farthest north institution of higher education. We saw the great gold dredges of the Fairbanks Exploration Company which rumbled away day and night during the summer digging up bucketsful of gold-bearing gravel and spewing out unsightly piles of tailings.

Joe's work accomplished, we started west on a sunny morning. Mt. McKinley reared up above the mist, a nebulous mass of pink, sun-tinged snow. Although in winter Alaska is a monotone of white and brown, in summer it is brilliantly colored. Meadows and muskeg are brightest emerald, timber varies from tender green of birch leaves to the darker spruce. Clumps of purple fireweed flame beside the trails. Salmon on drying racks are rawly red along the streams. Distant mountains are blue or lavendar in the haze.

A hill marked the railroad town of Nenana, where—although we didn't know it yet—we were to spend the long, cold winter. The Kantishna River, flowing north from the Alaska Range. Tolovana, with its excellent roadhouse. Then Manley Hot Springs where there was another splendid place to stay, and a spring of soft water which was warm the year round. Soft water was welcomed by people coming from Fairbanks where the water was hard and colored.

The muddy Tanana River merged with the mighty Yukon at Tanana, with its deserted buildings of old Fort Gibbon. Here was Alaska's great river which had headed only twenty miles from salt water back in Yukon Territory, which was still small at Whitehorse and Dawson, but growing with the addition of every tributary as it turned west and flowed on to empty at last into Bering Sea.

There were only occasional cabins along the river for the next hundred miles but during the winter our pilots would get to know each of them intimately when they were forced to land and deliver mail in a personal rural free delivery service such as the dog teams had given.

Ruby, on the left bank of the Yukon, was once a prosperous gold camp. We came in over a bluff rising sheer from the water, a fish wheel at its base. Malemute pups raced along the beach and a chorus of dogs howled a greeting, among them Mrs. Tom Devane's red setters which jumped up on their kennels and howled as if they were wolves. The malemute chorus was a typical Alaskan sound. On cold winter mornings I often woke up to the wolf-like howls and thought I was back on the Colorado prairie listening to the coyotes.

Once Ruby turned its back on the river, but a fire wiped out all of the frontage side of the street. Now Tom DeVane's new store was the most pretentious building in town. We climbed up to the rickety board walk through the summer's accumulation of garbage.

Breakfast that morning at an old roadhouse by the river was one of the few meals I have ever faced which I could not eat. The proprietor, an old 'sourdough', wore a floursack apron stiff with dirt and grease. When we came in he fired up his range, squirted tobacco juice on it from a plentiful cud in his cheek, and when the stove was hot enough so that the juice bounced, he rubbed off a place with his apron and poured on sourdough for hotcakes. I had been airsick, and my appetite did not return.

Joe made arrangements with Mrs. Verhonik, a pleasant, efficient-appearing woman, for servicing the planes during the coming winter.

Here in Ruby we encountered our first antagonism to the airplane from old timers who grieved because the dog team trails would not be kept open. Fresh from the 'outside' we had thought the speedier mail service would be an unmixed blessing. Now we discovered that the roadhouses along the river depended upon the mail drivers and the prices they paid for dog salmon to feed their teams.

Mildred Fisher, the cheery young postmistress, showed me around the town. Her family had just come down to Ruby from Seward, but before that they had owned a cafe in Dawson. She told me of Ruby's boom days. Now it was a ghost town with deep grass around the remaining empty cabins. The Catholic church was forlorn in the bushes. But Miss Fisher was certain the camp would 'come back'.

"All the streets were built up in the gold rush days. There were sidewalks back there which are gone now. We used to live back there several streets. Houses were built in solidly. Now they're all torn down. But we'll make a stake here. The mines will open again."

The Fishers were not really ready for business at the hotel which they were opening but we persuaded them to take us in overnight and enjoyed the luxury of a good—and clean—bed. We assured them their success would be well deserved, especially after eating a delicious meal cooked by Mr. Fisher.

Next morning we were off down the Yukon. From the north the Koyukuk River wound down to empty into the Yukon. In fifty-five minutes we came to Nulato, with the town on the north bank of the river, and a fish camp opposite, where salmon dried. At one end of the settlement were the mission buildings and at the other the graveyard hill. A kindly gray-haired priest, Father McElmeel, or 'Father Mac' as everyone affectionately called him, came to greet us, welcoming Joe back. It was here he had been nursed through the flu the winter before.

High piles of cordwood in front of the log cabins indicated the severity of Yukon winters. Old and young women and children sat on the river bank and smiled at us, whispering 'Cossack', their Russian word for white person.

O.P. Russell's trading post was our first stop. Mr. Russell gained fame among the pilots for his apple pies. A gasoline sign hung outside the building, advertising aviation gas. There was no automobile in town, "not even a bicycle" a small Indian boy informed us as he helped wheel gas down to the plane on a wheelbarrow. There was a small hospital in the town, and a radio station.

Alone I climbed the steep hill to the graveyard. It presented a gay appearance with tiny houses over the graves. Many were fenced and all were painted—blue, yellow, white. Green shrubs, blazing purple fireweed, blue lupines, all made a colorful scene. Over the graves fluttered flags, some new, some faded and torn. Mirrors were fastened to the flag poles. All bore crosses, some with names and some nameless. The names were largely Russian, as Nulato was first established by the Russians who, more than a hundred years before, were massacred by warring Indian tribes from the Koyukuk. Inside one of the little houses was a child's set of toy dishes.

The sweet-faced sisters prepared lunch for us at the mission and Father Mac showed us around the mission buildings. The church had a congregation of about 250 persons.

"On a winter Sunday," the priest said, smiling, "when the natives are dressed in fur mukluks and parkas I have added seventeen new odors to my category of smells."

Father Mac was a famous dog team driver. It was his dogs that Father Bernard Hubbard used in some of his expeditions, about which he wrote in his book, "Mush, You Malemutes".

Reverently the priest showed us volumes of hand-written manuscripts by the late Father Jette' of Tanana, a noted authority on the Indian languages. There were a dictionary, a geography, histories, handbooks of the legends and folk-lore of the tribes, research which comprised a life's work, all written in a copper plate script like print. These invaluable books were to be printed by the Smithsonian Institution.

In the afternoon we flew down the river to Kaltag. Here we saw a reindeer corral. We struck across the portage above the winter dog team trail, leaving the river to flow southwest in a great bend. Below us was treeless tundra. Then we were over the village of Unalakleet, which would be the western end of our Yukon mail line. It was built on a sand spit on Norton Sound. During the winter our planes would make this trip twice a week, bringing mail ten days from Seattle—instead of from three to four weeks.

On the banks of Unalakleet River were rack after rack of drying salmon, winter food for man and dog. We could smell the town before we landed. In a heavy fog, the pilots said, they had only to wind down the window and sniff to locate a Yukon River village in the summer time. But except for the fish offal by the racks, Unalakleet was a neat town. The missionary, a Lutheran, was an ardent gardener and from his example the natives each had a garden patch before their cabins. Unalakleet vegetables were known and prized all up and down Bering Sea Shores. I didn't then appreciate the rarity of a head of lettuce!

A funeral was in progress as we landed. Beside the church door stood crowds of Eskimoes, each woman wearing a shapeless coverall 'parka' of gingham, with a fur-trimmed hood at the back for carrying the inevitable black-eyed baby. They spoke some English. My childhood conception of Eskimoes living in igloos was meeting disillusionment. Wherever there had been a mission one found the Eskimoes or Indians living in cabins, speaking English. These seemed to be an intelligent, friendly people.

The teachers, Mr. and Mrs. Everett Neeley, invited us to their home for dinner. Their daughter Ellen, a curly-haired little girl, was the only white child in the village. We dined royally on roast duck, fresh spinach, fresh turnips (vegetables which were almost worth their weight in gold dust along this coast). The nurse was 'Outside' on vacation, but had left word to put up any infrequent visitors in her house so we slept in the tiny hospital, Mrs. Morton in the nurse's room, Joe and I on a folding davenport, and Mr. Morton on the hospital bed surrounded by an imposing array of instruments and medicines.

As we walked about the village we met a fat little Lapp lady whose husband was out in a reindeer camp. They had come to Unalakleet from Lapland to teach the Eskimoes the domestication of reindeer after Dr. Sheldon Jackson had introduced these animals into Alaska to replenish the meat supply of the Eskimo tribes. She was famous for her beautiful fur mukluks—skin boots—and parkas. Garments she made accompanied the Byrd Antarctic expedition. The following winter the children and I proudly wore the fur boots with checkered trimming, bright tassels, and turned-up Lapp toes which she made for us.

Mrs. Neeley decided to accompany us to Nome because she wanted to get a permanent wave.

As we flew along Norton Sound we saw driftwood piled like tepees along the coast. Here every stick of wood is precious and

71

this was distined for winter fuel. Once we saw a grave on a raised platform.

At Egawik there was a reindeer corral and packing plant belonging to the Lomen Corporation of Nome, which shipped reindeer meat commercially.

There was another cold storage plant and some reindeer butchering pens and slaughter houses at Shaktolik, where we landed and had lunch with one of the two white women there.

The Froskland's home was on a windswept sandspit bright at that season with Iceland poppies and small blue flowers. It was an attractive home with green-painted kitchen, a piano strewn with sheets of Chopin, a woven Finnish hanging of conventional reindeer—a comfortable home in an isolated land.

Mr. Froskland spoke of the reindeer industry as epitomizing the romance and adventure of a far-away country. In the early 1900's the small steamer *Bear* transported Siberian reindeer into Alaska, about 1280 in all. These were to be the nucleus of herds which would provide a permanent meat supply to the Eskimoes of western Alaska who had seen their seal herds depleted by ruthless slaughtering. In the thirty years since the first reindeer came to the tundra it was said that they had multiplied far beyond expectations so that now almost every village had a herd. By 1928 it was estimated that there were nearly a million reindeer foraging for themselves—and the tundra could provide space for many more. The Eskimoes had changed from hunter to herder where they had these animals.

In the air again, flying above the camp of Bonanza, of Moses—minus the bulrushes. Then we turned out over Bering Sea. Breakers spread, lace-edged, on the sand. Countless birds wheeled before the cliffs. Elim, Golovin, Bluff, Solomon—all tiny camps. Flags bordered a field where Wiley Post and Gatty had landed on their round-the-world flight. Then there was Safety Bay and at last ahead of us was Nome.

Nome, the city founded by gold—the many thousands of miners now gone leaving a huddle of gray, paintless buildings scattered along the beach.

We landed in Nome River beside the deserted buildings of Fort Davis—it appeared that all Army posts were presently abandoned. The road to town led past huts belonging to the Eskimoes who made up part of Nome's permanent population. One shack was made of flattened coaloil cans; another had clean, ruffled curtains at the windows. The occupants came out to watch us go past. They were mostly short and stocky, with Oriental features. The women wore calico parkas with a wide ruffle at the bottom, and with a fur-trimmed hood which often held a black-eyed baby. Their feet were shod variously with mocassins, mukluks, or high-heeled slippers. The men were also garbed in assorted fashion, some in store clothes and shoes, some with canvas parkas, some with seal-gut raincoats sewn in strips which went round and round. These raincoats, when wet, had a strong, fishy odor.

A group of King Islanders had just arrived from their barren, rocky island in the middle of Bering Sea. Apparently most of the island's population migrated every summer to Nome across eighty-five miles of open ocean in frail skin boats called 'umiaks'. They camped on the beach and the men found work in town or spent their summers carving ivory curios—paper knives, cribbage boards, bracelets, billikens. Their workshop was the shelter of the over-turned umiaks. With the money earned during the season, they bought their winter's supply of food and returned before freeze-up to their bleak island and their huts of skin and bone perched precariously on rocky cliffs.

During our stay in Nome, Eskimoes also arrived from the Diomede Islands, our farthest west possessions—today we possess only Little Diomede and Russia owns Big Diomede and there is no free communication between them. The Diomeders lived in tents and also worked under their umiaks making lovely beads and bracelets of ancient mastodon ivory. I enjoyed going out to the sandspit where I could watch them at their skillful carving. To drill holes in a walrus tusk for a cribbage board one old man held the drill against a board between his teeth and revolved it by a strung bow.

I was told that Eskimoes from East Cape, Siberia, often also came to Nome for supplies. Yet anthropologists sometimes talked as if a former Bering Strait land bridge had been necessary to explain how North America became inhabited.

To me, the Eskimoes were the most interesting thing in Nome. Without them it would have been a dreary place, surrounded by spongy, treeless tundra. The soil was so sour that there were no gardens, no vegetables. It rained, or fog blanketed the town every day for two weeks.

Once Nome had a population of 20,000—or perhaps even 30,000 inhabitants; now there were six or seven hundred people in the summer and less during the winter. Deserted buildings leaned at crazy, tipsy angles. The board sidewalks had sunk or warped as the ground heaved or settled with the frosts. There was no plumbing or sanitation in the whole city. Garbage and refuse were dumped on the beach—on sands which once yielded millions of dollars in gold—and twice a year the ice scoured it away. Contents of the 'chemical' toilets were gathered each day in a 'honey cart' and hauled away.

Only a few ships came into Bering Sea during the summer. There were no docks because the Sea was shallow for some distance offshore, so the ships anchored a mile or so out from shore and freight and passengers were lightered in. Everything was in short supply until a ship came with the winter's goods. There were no magazines to buy, and I could not even get film for my camera.

Yet we soon found comfortable, well-furnished homes and within them was the proverbial Alaskan hospitality.

CHAPTER EIGHT
Flight Around Alaska

The radio operator received word that Charles and Anne Lindbergh had left Point Barrow on their flight 'north to the Orient' and were on their way to Nome. Joe and I went to the radio station to listen for Mrs. Lindbergh's signals. Their plane was equipped with radio and she was the operator.

It began to grow dark while they were still in the air. Darkness was coming back over the northland after the summer's period of long daylight. Joe went out to Nome River to direct setting out flares so that the Colonel could see to land. Nome River is narrow at its best, and an after-dark landing would be a tricky business. Everyone was relieved when the radio message came that they were landing on a lagoon for the night and would continue to Nome in the morning.

Our sleeping quarters were in a room above the bank, directly over the main street. All night we heard the soft shuffle of mocassined feet on the board sidewalks and found the next morning that the Eskimoes had stayed up all night waiting to greet the 'Little Blue Goose' as they called Mrs. Lindbergh. This was an affectionate title; it seems that the blue goose is one of the rarest of migratory fowl, and ranges the farthest afield.

The fog rolled out to sea the next morning and the whole town was on the street to watch the trim, low-wing Lockheed soar overhead and fly eastward to a landing on Safety Bay.

The banker and his wife turned out of their own apartment at the rear of the bank to make room for the town's distinguished guests. That evening we visited them. Joe and Colonel Lindbergh sat in a corner on the davenport and discussed engines—they were each flying the same type of new model engine and Joe's had been causing trouble. I tried to draw Joe away.

"Oh, let them talk," Mrs. Lindbergh begged. "It is so seldom Charles gets to talk to another man who speaks the same language."

Colonel Lindbergh was technical advisor for Pan American Airways, and for a long time Joe had been interested in that company. For years it had been his dream to build an air route across the Pacific. The Colonel gave him names of men in New York who might be interested in our Alaskan operation. That talk on the couch in a Nome apartment led to the eventual coming of

75

Pan American Airways to Alaska, and thus indirectly to Joe's one day becoming the captain of a China Clipper flying to the Orient.

Next day brought rain and we, and perforce the Lindberghs, stayed over. During the afternoon the Eskimoes entertained with water sports during which the chief and two other men raced in their frail kayaks. These were tiny boats covered with skin except for one hole into which the men climbed. Raincoats were tied around the opening so that the craft was water-tight. After the races the chief turned his kayak upside down in the breakers and then righted it.

The Arctic Brotherhood Hall was bright with lights that night when the Eskimoes performed the Wolf Dance, the first time—so we heard—that it had been put on since 1914. The hall was crowded. We sat on benches in the center of the room. There was standing-room only with Eskimoes crowding around the sides and on the balcony.

The rear of the stage was covered with beautiful furs, silky polar bear skins. Women in glossy reindeer parkas formed a sort of chorus at the rear of the stage. In each hand they held a long feather, which they moved gracefully in time to the music. The 'orchestra' was down in front, a semi-circle of old men in white drill parkas, slapping flat skin drums with the palms of their hands. They sang a monotonous chant over and over, slowly at first and then as the movements of the dancers quickened, they pounded in faster and faster tempo until the rhythm throbbed into the blood as if it were laden with some ancestral meaning.

Five men were on the stage, in front of a sort of platform in which there were five round holes which were supposed to represent wolves' dens. At first the dancers wore white shirts, trousers and mukluks, with gauntlets trimmed with auk's bills which clattered together as they moved their arms in unison. The chief was in the center of the stage. The dancers worked up their steps in pitch and excitement until, at a sudden movement, they disappeared into the holes behind them. A moment later five wolves' heads looked out of the holes, moving this way and that. Then the dancers appeared, wearing the wolves' heads and swaying about the platform on all fours, animal-like grace in their movements which kept time to the pound of the old men's drums. Then with one sudden spring, they disappeared backwards into the holes again.

Many of the early missionaries tried to put a stop to native dances, in whatever culture, and of course many of these dances did have a religious significance which was naturally 'pagan' and therefore abhorrent to the men of God. But taking away of the old dances helped to destroy cultures, traditions, folk-lore until the

76

'natives' began to think that their own heritage was something of which to be ashamed. I'm glad that today enlightened anthropologists are encouraging people to preserve their old folk-ways, and hope that it isn't too late. Much has been forgotten and is gone forever.

After the dance the Eskimoes engaged in competitive sports, one of which was kicking a skin ball hanging from the rafters, kicking with both feet together. The young men would double up and kick upward, then land with both feet on the floor. One little girl, braids swinging, kicked up with both feet considerably higher than her head. After this event a huge walrus skin was brought in and held tautly by the young Eskimoes and anyone who wished was tossed up in 'the blanket'. The idea was to land upon one's feet. This was perhaps the beginning of the modern trampoline.

Never shall I forget that close-packed hall, the throb of the skin drums, the chant of the old men singers, or the sight of the leaping figures on the stage in dance forms so ancient the meaning was all but lost.

Joe had been negotiating to buy out the Northern Air Transport, a Nome-based company, of which Mr. Oliver was the president. But while we were in Nome he received a telegram saying that the mother of Mr. Lowe, our partner and financial backer, had died. All of her estate was tied up and there would be no more money forthcoming for expansion, or indeed for actual operation.

There was no longer any need for us to stay in Nome.

But before we left Mr. Oliver pointed out the 'ruby sand' along the beach where in the early days of the mining camps fortunes had been made. This seemed an opportunity to swell the family funds so he loaned me a gold pan and shovel and I went to work. After shaking out two pans of gravel with infinite care I was rewarded with three infintisimal specks of gold, worth possibly a fraction of a cent, and gave up the labor as too strenuous for the results obtained.

Shortly after we came to Anchorage Margie Lou and Teddy had been stimulated by the talk of gold into panning dirt beside the sidewalk under our apartment windows. They had better results as Teddy found a dime. The youngsters of the neighborhood, hearing of this phenomenal strike, nearly tore up the wooden sidewalks, but there didn't seem to be any more pay dirt.

A sunny morning arrived at last and we prepared to leave. I flew with Joe from the Nome River over to Safety Bay where we would load our passengers; in addition to the attorney and his wife, the postal inspector was going part way with us. We landed beside the Lindbergh's plane where it rode at anchor, and while ours was being gassed up I watched Mrs. Lindbergh working with her radio.

From Nome they were heading across Bering Sea to Kamchatka.

At one-thirty we were off, with Bering Sea smooth and blue on our right, clouds making patterns of sunshine and shadow on the green tundra below. Stakes marked the winter mail trail, the only landmarks, when the world was snowcovered, to keep a dogteam driver on his course. The landscape was a symphony of blues on lagoons, ocean, distant hills, and paler sky. The schoolbuildings of the White Mountain Industrial School stood out against a green hill.

The inspector had to stop at Golovin to inspect the post office, so we landed in front of the corrugated tin buildings of the Lomen Commercial Store on Golovin Bay. The trader's wife fixed lunch for us in her sunny home, one equipped with running water from a big tank in the kitchen. In addition to this real luxury she had a bathtub and an electric plant.

Beyond Golovin we cut across to the Lomen reindeer camp and saw a herd of deer being driven toward the corrals. The hills were brown with the moving herds. What a wonderful idea it was to bring these animals to the tundra world. Where is there another animal so versatile, one that furnishes food, shelter, clothing and transportation? Reindeer hides make parkas, trousers, mukluks and tents. Reindeer meat is a staple food which was being processed for shipment south to 'the States'. The Laplanders also tamed the animals and hitched them to sleds.

When we landed at Unalakleet we found that Mrs. Froskland from Shaktolik was there. This swelled the white population to four women and naturally made an occasion for a dance. We all went up to the big room over Mr. Traeger's trading post and someone started a phonograph.

One of our aviators was stranded in Unalakleet and was glad to see us land. He had made a forced landing on the tundra thirty miles overland, on pontoons, and had hiked to the coast. Next morning he added his luggage to ours and climbed aboard.

South of Unalakleet to the mouth of the Yukon was a lonely coast line, broken only by an Indian camp or two and tripods of driftwood stacked out of reach of the waves.

We landed in the bay at St. Michael, taxied to shore and tied up to the hull of an old river boat. The beach was strewn with the remains of boats, pulled up and left to rot—mute evidences of Alaska's former glory.

St. Michael was built by the Russians in 1833. Logs used for the original buildings were brought all the way from Sitka, over a thousand miles to the south. On a point was a little blockhouse with its two fat cannons—one of them lying rusting in the grass. There was a bathhouse, an old log house, the sod ice house, and the Greek Catholic Church, all dating back to Russian occupation.

An Indian boy brought a key and opened the church. Its onion-shaped dome and triple cross are a familiar sight in this part of Alaska. Within was dust and mold but there were priceless ikons and paintings supposedly as lovely as those in the famous church at Sitka. I saw a Russian Bible, and one purchased from Montgomery Ward. Only rarely did a visiting priest come this way to hold services in the old church. It required a great stretch of the imagination to picture the building full of devout worshipers.

Once St. Michael was a very important port. Here came ships from Seattle bringing goods that were transferred to river steamers which journeyed up the Yukon River nearly two thousand miles to Dawson and Whitehorse. All the freight for the Klondike came this way, unless it was carried on men's backs over the White Pass or the Chilkoot. Then the building of the White Pass & Yukon Railroad took away much of the necessity for the long journey to St. Michael.

I walked down to the wharves. There were great warehouses built for busy days. Now the warehouses were empty, the wharves were rotting, and the river boats were pulled up on the beach, abandoned.

Still later a United States fort was built and a troop of soldiers was garrisoned here. We walked about the quadrangle of the fort buildings, now empty and echoing.

Board walks straggled off across the tundra, leading nowhere, becoming lost in the grass. The trading post had some beautiful Nunivak Island baskets at ridiculously low prices. The nurse in the little infirmary was the only white woman living in St. Michael, one of fifteen or sixteen persons who made up the permanent population. During its hundred years or more of existence the place was first an Indian village, then a Russian fortress; the gold rush made it a boom town.. After this a United States Army post was maintained, and now it is an Indian village again.

One of the funniest stories I ever read—and it wasn't intended to be funny—had the setting in St. Michael. It was written by a leading author and published in a popular weekly which is no longer in existence. However, the author had never been in St. Michael and probably not anywhere in all Alaska from his glaring errors. He had a jail break take place in the story, with bullets riccocheting from the pavement—there were only a few board walks here. He had automobiles drawn up at the curb—there was no curb, and there were no automobiles closer than Nome. The hero telephoned to the airport for one of our planes—that publicity was all right—but there were no telephones, no airport, and our planes landed there only on radio call. The hero planned to take a

79

scheduled flight directly to 'the States'. Someday there might be such a service from St. Michael but those days were—then at least—far in the rosy future. And as climax, the hero, having an hour or two to wait, debated over which of the two movies he should see and decided on a 'talkie' at the Criterion. I doubt if there had then ever been a movie in St. Michael—and as for two theaters! Well, the story had imagination and originality. I can say that it certainly was original! But it showed the importance of knowing whereof one speaks or writes. Yet I doubt if anyone in the United States, reading the magazine, ever questioned any of the details of the story.

Our next stage of the flight took us over some of the most lonely land on the earth's surface, between the deltas of the Yukon and the Kuskokwin Rivers. There were three or four little hills with craters in the top, the only landmarks in the wide tundra. We crossed the Yukon at Andreafski and beyond was bare tundra with here and there a reindeer herd grazing. There was room in Alaska for many more reindeer than Texas ever had cattle—meat in 'Uncle Sam's icebox'. The few Indians living here had the most primitive conditions of any to be found in Alaska and were the least touched by 'civilization'.

There was not a moment when the plane could not have landed safely for there were lakes and streams everywhere but walking out over the muskeg—ah! that's the rub. Then ahead was the Kuskokwim, Alaska's second big waterway, with Bethel sprawled on the bank.

We landed in the muddy river and pulled up to the beach. At one end of the village was a fox farm. Green-painted buildings of the Moravian mission were set in a large garden, and huge marigolds bloomed around the house. There was a bare, shabby church, completely unattractive—and I couldn't help thinking of the lovely ikons in the deserted one at St. Michael. Most of the Indian's cabins were small and unpainted. At that time there were about twenty white people in Bethel, five families and a few prospectors.

The big Northern Commercial Company store was fascinating with the wide variety of its stock. The N.C. was to interior Alaska what the Hudson's Bay posts were to northern Canada. On the shelves together were Murine for the eyes, liquid veneer, shaving cream, drugs, fox medicines, candy, root beer, cheap jewelry, ivory cribbage boards, phonograph records, shoes, Nunivak baskets, overalls, mocassins, red and white fox furs, anything and everything. In another room were two pool tables and a motion picture projector. A bulletin announced that Saturday night Buddy Rogers and Mary Brian would be seen in a picture. So the movies had come to western Alaska—but this little room was hardly a

*Margie Lou and Teddy admiring
native art at Ketchikan, 1931*

Pier at Valdez—long before the devastating earthquake

Pacific International Airways fleet at Merrill Field, Anchorage before the winter mail runs began

Father McElmeel at Nulato

Nome before the fire. 1931

Charles Lindbergh and author at Nome on their flight "North to the Orient", summer 1931

Visiting with Anne Lindbergh

The flying Barrows family at Nenana

Wives of the pilots based at Nenana, (L. to R.) Mrs. Valley, Cope, McGee, Holden and Barrows. Teddy and Margie Lou in front

With Dan Green's dog team at Manley Hot Springs, one of the regular mail stops

"Criterion Theater".

We were invited to dinner at the home of the trader and his wife. This was my first meeting with Dixie and Esther Hall, who were to be my very good neighbors later in Fairbanks. His southern accent had won the trader the name of 'Dixie' and whenever I remember him I think of a Christmas Eve a few years later in Fairbanks. The temperature was about fifty degrees below zero and most of the youth of Fairbanks were assembled in the Presbyterian Church to have their annual Christmas tree treat. I was shepherding my Sunday School class of little girls and the boys' class—including my son and Dixie's two little boys—was seated in the pew directly in front of me.

Amid a great ringing of sleigh bells, Santa Claus opened the front door and came in with a cloud of vapor from the cold outside air. He ran up on the platform, turned and smiled at the children and greeted them with a hearty,

"Merry Christmas to you-all."

Barbee Hall turned to me and whispered, "Don't tell who it is; maybe some of the little kids won't know it's Dad." But that southern accent surely gave away the identity of Santa Claus.

The Hall's home on the Kuskokwim was a pleasant building, with cretonne-curtained windows framing a view of the river and the tundra beyond.

We spent the night at a roadhouse where the beds were of dubious cleanliness, and the next afternoon struck across the tundra to Quinhagak. Reindeer grazed on the slopes all the way to the Auhlun Mountains—how widely had Dr. Sheldon Jackson's first few animals spread! The plane crossed the peninsula from Goodnews Bay to Togiak Bay and ahead were the bright waters of Bristol Bay. Over the Mishagak Peninsula to Nushagak Bay—how I love those names! Unalakleet, Quigiligmute, Napiamute, Akiak, Kuskokwim, Kantishna, Kanakanak—and with every one comes an associated memory picture.

The treeless tundra was changing to mountain scenery with jagged, saw-peaked hills where depressions like little cups held blue lakes. A prospector's camp was on a lonely stream, his boat drawn up nearby.

In Bristol Bay were the big canneries of Nushagak. We stopped at the green-painted buildings of the Kanakanak Industrial School in a clean, pretty village, landing at the foot of the hill. Then we flew over to Dillingham and taxied up onto the beach. Joe carefully supervised tying up of the plane, as a few weeks before a pilot had looked out from the trading post to see his float plane going out with the tide and had to commandeer a boat to go to rescue it.

A widow owned the trading post, the restaurant, and the

cannery boats. Her pretty sister, a student at the University of Washington, was spending the summer helping in the trading post, practicing the native tongue in dealing with the native fishermen and their wives. This had been a Russian settlement a hundred years ago and a cannery town for a long time, but the natives talked only their native tongue. The most used phrase sounded like "nah-ma-gi-ca." "I don't know." A trading jargon was used almost entirely in the store.

In the cannery towns salmon was king during the fishing season. In the short period of the salmon run the Indian fishermen would earn their winter's food and necessities. Fishermen from 'outside' hoped for a big run to pay for bringing their boats so far. Cannery workers scaled and cut fish around the clock for the canning machines. Then suddenly it would all be over. The cases of canned salmon would be loaded aboard ships. The cannery workers would drift away. The fishing boats would be tied up. Only a watchman would be left at the cannery until time to get the machinery ready for another year.

Above the town was a cemetery with old Russian graves, triple crosses over them leaning lipsily in the tall grass. We were hospitably invited to spend the night in comfortable rooms over the trading post.

Off again on a sunny Sunday morning, along the Nushagak River and north to Illiamna Lake, a beautiful sheet of water with snow-capped mountains rising from the rim. It had begun to rain and the pass was fogged in, so we landed to sit out the storm on the lake. It was a pretty place to camp, but we had no equipment and when we stepped out on the pontoons the mosquitoes attacked in ravenous hordes. Within an hour the rain stopped, the clouds lifted, and we threaded our way through the narrow pass and came out over Cook Inlet.

Canneries offered emergency stopping places if we needed to come down. Our gas supply was running low but Joe continued on up the Inlet, carefully calculating the distance home. Both wing tanks were dry and the engine was running on the center section tank when we saw Turnagain Arm ahead—named by Captain Cook in his northern explorations. Then Knik Arm and the neat streets of Anchorage. As Joe circled I saw Teddy run out of Blunt's house, a little red dot in his knit suit.

We had been gone a month and I was pleased to have seen so much of Alaska in that time. Anchorage looked like a metropolis after the little native villages and trading posts where we had stopped. As we settled back into our rather drab little apartment I was able to appreciate the luxury of a bathroom. Plumbing had been conspicuously lacking all along our route. I also appreciated the fact that the weekly train, connecting at Seward with the Alaska Steamship line from Seattle, brought us weekly mail and fresh vegetables—never again to be taken entirely for granted.

Years later, during the Korean War, I was on Kwajalein atoll in the Marshall Islands. I remember telling someone that living on this tropical island had much in common with life in Alaska in the early days. Questioned about this statement, I told how we had also then depended upon the ships to bring us mail and fresh food and how we had hoarded a head of lettuce—making it last as long as possible.

It was necessary for Joe to leave at once for the 'Outside' as Mr. Lowe wanted to sell the company before the beginning of the mail contracts in November. His family had put up the performance bonds of $140,000 and the estate was to be settled after his mother's death. Or, if the company could not be sold in that year of deep depression, Joe had to try to get equipment and money for hangar facilities and spare motors and materials for the long, hard winter which was ahead. In the meantime, pilots and mechanics in Anchorage continued their charter freight and passenger business, not knowing from one week to the next whether they would be out of a job.

When I received word from Fairbanks that the house we had rented was now vacant, I decided to go up there, unpack our furniture, and begin really keeping house again. We weren't certain how long we would be in Alaska, but we did know that the November first deadline was coming nearer and nearer when the mail contracts must be started.

I called the depot to get a train schedule and was informed that they were not sure whether the train would run Wednesday or Saturday. One got used to the vagaries of the Alaska Railroad. Eventually it left on a Wednesday and, as it was not a boat train, I had the passenger car practically to myself. This was good because the children—who had traveled thousands of miles by air—had never before ridden on a train and they had to investigate window catches and the working of the shades and the drinking fountains.

The train stopped for the night at Curry. An old prospector sat at our table in the luxurious dining room—maybe not luxurious in comparison with the Miami-Biltmore, but certainly in comparison with roadhouses along the Yukon. He grinned every time he looked at the children, and kept watching them intently. I apologized for their table manners, which were far from perfect, but he assured me that they didn't annoy him.

"I haven't seen any white children for years," he said. No wonder they were interesting, as healthy young specimens of the species.

As we crossed the railroad bridge over the Tanana River at Nenana a man pointed down into the water.

"I lost sixty thousand dollars right down there last spring," he told me solemnly.

I wasn't yet enough of an Alaskan to understand what he meant and thought wildly that he must have dropped his wallet overboard and wondered why he carried such a fabulous sum. Then he told me that this was the place where the ice pool stake was driven in the Tanana River ice and that when it went out with the ice in the spring it carried with it the hopes of those who had tried to guess the exact minute it would move. Since then I've also lost sixty thousand dollars or more under the bridge.

In the evening we came to Fairbanks, where we got a room at the Nordale Hotel. Then we walked along Front Street to look at the house where we were to live. A soft light came from the log cabins along the way, lamplight shining on the early October snow. Across the slough sounded the bell of the Catholic church, ringing at six o'clock. Somewhere a malemute howled, and soon there was a chorus of dogs answering.

Before we could move into our house a plumber had to refill the radiators and keep a fire long enough to be sure that water was circulating and that icy rooms were warming. Then trucks brought our crated furniture and we began to feel at home.

When I asked my landlord for a key for the front door he said, "There never has been a key for that door. Here in Alaska we don't lock our doors."

At first I propped a chair under the knob at night then gradually forgot to do so. But one night I was awakened by a terrific crash which sounded as if an army was trying to get in through the coal chute. Trembling, I began to steal down the stairs to phone the police when I heard the sound again and saw a huge chunk of snow sliding past the windows, to crash beside the house. If you've ever heard snow sliding from a tin roof in the middle of the night, you know what a sound it makes.

The children got whooping cough at once and for a month they whooped and vomited, growing thin and pale. There was no sun, so I gave them cod liver oil.

All the time I was engaged in a battle with the coal furnace. I spent most of my time shoveling coal. The temperature wasn't dreadfully low, thirty below zero perhaps, but hour after hour, day and night, I shoveled coal. The floors were cold, the kitchen was cold; food froze in the pantry. Five tons of coal I burned in one month, and then the house wasn't warm. The foundations hadn't been properly banked and too much heat escaped.

When Joe left in August he had expected to be gone three

weeks, but his letters were a continual chronicle of failure. It was impossible, in this depression year, to sell a business requiring an outlay of $140,000 for the performance bonds, in addition to capital required for hangars and equipment. He went from New York to Baltimore and from Washington to Buffalo with no success. Days dragged into weeks, and then into months.

The Post Office Department said we would be forced to carry out the dog team schedule, which meant making all of the way stops with airplanes, exactly as the dog teams had done. This was a rural free delivery service, to be run by air. And the first of November was upon us, with no extra planes, no hangars, nothing.

CHAPTER NINE

Pioneering Air Mail in Alaska

Alaska was not yet prepared for air mail. The dog team had played a major, and romantic, part in Arctic transportation. When the short summer was over and the rivers froze, the dogs had been important in freight and passenger service. The loaded sleds could average about twenty miles a day, and along the river trails roadhouses—usually only cabins offering shelter and a little food at exorbitant prices—were spaced to accommodate this slow-moving travel. The dog teams kept the trails open. The mail teams broke trail after each snow storm while other travelers waited beside fires until the mail driver mushed past.

These travelers, these roadhouse keepers, these trappers living in isolated cabins, wanted their trails kept open, and they issued a howl which reached Washington, D.C. The airplane would break no trails; it would eat no dried fish which the roadhouse keepers stored to sell to dogteam drivers. Now the Post Office Department said the planes must land at each isolated mail box along the river.

The P.I.A. had expected adequate financial backing for these 3200 miles of weekly flights—with 83 stops per week—at the time they bid on the contracts. They had planned for small planes to carry the way mail and for a steam-heated hangar at Fairbanks. Now the men didn't know from one day to the next whether the company would be sold over their heads, leaving them jobless.

The P.I.A. had only four planes. One had been landed on the tundra in August and it was still there, waiting for snowfall so that skis could be mounted to fly it out.

Two of the planes, a Bellanca and a model-71 Wasp-motored Fairchild, were busy with weekly freight and passenger service from Anchorage to the Kuskokwim and Bristol Bay. This was a cash business averaging $6000 a month, and if the planes were required to base 300 miles north at Fairbanks this profitable business must be abandoned.

And on the first of November, taking off on the first mail flight, the fourth ship gathered ice on the wings and crashed on the Fairbanks airport. It was in the shop six weeks for overhaul.

A charter plane was hired, with pilot, to start the mail. But the river ice was unsafe for landings the first month; fall storms set in, and it was impossible to maintain a schedule. Mail which could not be carried piled up in the post offices along the route. The chartered plane dropped through the ice at Unalakleet. Mail service went farther behind. Complaints poured in. At some anti-airplane roadhouses signs were put up

'If you want to kick about the mail service
do it here. We'll see that your complaints
reach Washington, D.C.'

Dog teams were then hired to haul the way mail as far as Ruby. But even dog teams could not keep schedules in the soft snow. And all of the revenue was going to pay for hired airplanes and dog teams.

The Anchorage freight business had to be abandoned. The planes were brought up to Nenana and operations were concentrated there. Nenana was sixty miles below Fairbanks and even sixty miles of flying time was important on short winter days. A shed built of wall board was thrown up on the river ice, where motors could be checked. Here the mechanics, Loren Fernald, Jinks Ames, and Larry Davis could service the motors out of the wind—but not out of the cold. A fire going full blast in the stove could be felt only a few feet away. I saw the thermometer, hanging on a two-by-four only three feet above the stove register 30 degrees below zero one morning—and the stove was red hot.

By the middle of November the days were so short it took an entire week to make one Kuskokwim trip to Bethel and back, or one down the Yukon and across to Unalakleet and back, yet our schedule called for two round trips a week to Unalakleet and one to Bethel. The complaints increased—no one was satisfied with the poor mail service, and they couldn't be blamed.

In Fairbanks bets were placed that the P.I.A. could not last until the first of the year. There were no takers; it looked completely hopeless.

Wages were not paid. The gas company refused to give additional credit. Morale was low. The men felt that the whole project was a failure, and their jobs were insecure.

This was the situation Joe found when he returned from New York with a prospective buyer. The buyer took one look and left—probably deciding to wait for the failure and then perhaps step in and buy up the pieces.

During this time I was in Fairbanks with the children. The house we had rented was a Jonah and I was spending most of my time shoveling coal in a vain attempt to keep it warm.

Joe and I held an emergency session and decided it was foolish to keep up the house with the high coal bills. Since he would have to be in Nenana for the balance of the winter I would go down there, too. I again put the furniture in storage, packed two suitcases of clothing, and caught the weekly train down to Nenana with my pale, thin little youngsters who were just recovering from the severe attacks of whooping cough.

We rented two bedrooms in the front of the second floor of the Southern Hotel, where we had an uninterrupted view of anything moving on Main Street. It was a relief to have steam heat for which I wasn't responsible. There was even a bathroom in the hotel, though the water was hard and we had to pay fifty cents to take a bath. We filled water pitchers at a tap in the hall, and washed in bowls sitting upon old-fashioned commodes in our rooms.

The hotel had no fire escapes. Instead a coil of rope was tied to a nail beneath the window, which was securely closed for the winter and had a storm window nailed on the outside. Ventilation came through three small holes bored in the storm sash. One night I heard the cry of "Fire" and ran into the next room to get the children. It was 50 degrees below zero outside. I had visions of sliding down the rope with a child under each arm and landing in the snowbank below. But someone put out the fire and I didn't have to test my acrobatic ability.

Two other pilot's wives, Margaret Cope and Lorraine Holden, spent part of the winter at the Southern Hotel with us. They taught me to play bridge. Lorraine also knew thirteen kinds of solitaire.

The lower part of the hotel contained a huge dance hall which was an excellent playroom for Margie Lou and Teddy. The depot agent's children, also under school age, sometimes came to play with them. I began to teach Margie Lou the regular first grade work and we conducted school every morning. I also sent 'outside' for kindergarten materials for Teddy.

There were seventeen of the P.I.A. personnel registered at the hotel. We ate at a restaurant across the street, where the food was excellent but sadly lacking in salads and fresh vegetables. The best thing about our living arrangements was that both the restaurant keeper and the hotel landlady let us all run a bill until the mail checks began coming.

Finances were indeed desperate. All revenue was going to the dog teams and chartered planes. No one had been paid for months. Joe called the staff together and put the situation up to them frankly. The company might be sold any time and then we would all be jobless. Now the men were free to quit and look for other positions. If they stayed they'd have hard work, under adverse conditions, and might not get paid for months. One pilot quit and so did one Anchorage mechanic. They were immediately hired by another company. The rest stayed.

This talk turned the tide. Now there was something to fight for. Our backs were against the wall, everyone expected us to fail. But we'd show 'em. It might be a short fight but it would be a good one while it lasted. More or less profanely each man said,

"Joe, I'm no quitter. I'll stick by you. I don't give a damn about those performance bonds, but if you're going to fight it out I'll help."

A new spirit was born, and the P.I.A. dug in.

The Anchorage office was closed, cutting off all cash revenue for slow-pay mail. In January the first mail check arrived and was used to pay November's bills for dog teams and chartered plane. The first rented plane was dismissed in December and a smaller one hired to make way stops for three weeks until the mail was caught up. The dog teams were dismissed. Bob Busby had been driving one of them. Since that time Bob won permanent trophies in the Fairbanks dog derbies as one of Alaska's best drivers. We kidded him about learning to race dogs when he was "mushing with the air mail."

December twentieth the disabled Fairchild came back into service from the Fairbanks shops.

Pilot Lon Cope, with an Eskimo helper named Elijah, went out for the old 51 Fairchild grounded on the tundra near Unalakleet. This was the same plane we had flown to New York and back in 1929. Working in a heavy gale at sub-zero temperatures, Lon and Elijah took off the pontoons and fitted on the skis. Gas was used up breaking a runway in the soft snow by taxiing back and forth so Elijah had to go to Unalakleet for more gas and food. For weeks a heavy coast fog and storms kept Lon grounded as those planes were radioless and he could get no weather reports.

While Lon was isolated his wife went to the hospital where their son was born, and died, with no way of contacting the father. Finally Frank Dorbrandt, on a trip to Nome, circled over and dropped Lon a note. Lon was determined to take off regardless of weather. He broke a tail ski in taxiing out a runway so he tied a shovel on in its place, took off, and landed at Unalakleet with about a pint of gas left in the tanks. Without stopping to repair the tail ski, he picked up a load of incoming mail and flew up the river to Nenana, arriving on Christmas Day.

Father McElmeel, the genial priest at the Nulato mission, used to take hot coffee down to the cold and weary pilots when they landed at Nulato. He told about it afterward.

"You might know fellows like that would succeed," he said, chuckling. "They wouldn't stop to eat, or to rest, or even to get warm. Why, if they broke a tail ski they just tied on a shovel and kept flying!"

Now all four planes were back on the job and the last week of December all the back mail was cleaned up. Joe went on regular flying duty to replace the pilot who had quit and he flew every minute of daylight, then sat up half the night working on the books and management details when he was in Nenana. One big task was to write letters which would make the partner—wintering in a comfortable apartment in California—understand just what they were doing to save his performance bonds. After all, the hard-working employees were getting nothing out of this, personally or financially, except the satisfaction of doing a job which everyone had said couldn't be done.

The gas company, watching the men's efforts, agreed to extend credit and take pay from the mail checks when they arrived.

Overhead was cut to the bone. The Anchorage office secretary had been dismissed and I took over the flight reports so there was no expense for office work. There was no hangar rent to pay. The men worked sixteen hours a day, dropping into bed dog-tired at night. Long before belated daylight they were down on the river ice in the deep cold with firepots going under the motors and fire extinguishers in hand in case the long, greasy motor coverings caught fire. Mail was loaded and planes took off at the first moment of precious daylight.

When the planes returned at dark and the pilots climbed wearily up the river bank, mail bills in hand, and sank down by a fire too tired and cold to move, the mechanics still worked. Night after night, until all hours, in the bitter cold they serviced those motors and gave them top overhauls so they would not be out of the air a moment of daylight—for in winter Alaskan days are only a few hours long.

During that six months every plane came in under its own power. The motors were run and run and run. They couldn't be taken out of service for overhauls but must keep going, without even a spare part or propellor in reserve. Twice motor covers caught fire and burned the ignition wires, each time on an outbound trip—but the plane finished the trip. Once a plane went through the tide-affected ice at Unalakleet, but that meant only a day or two of delay. There was not an accident all winter. Such a record speaks for itself, speaks for the quality of the pilots and for the quality of the mechanics.

A year later when Pan American Airways had bought us out and Lyman Peck became the new manager he said that every man in the company was taken over into the new service by his own record—"a record such as those men made last winter is the finest kind of recommendation."

In February Alex Holden left to take his wife 'outside' to the hospital. Joe, Al Monsen, and Lon Cope were left to finish up the mail contracts. A regular schedule was maintained 100% during the remainder of the season.

That winter of 1931-32 was one of the worst on record. Snow piled higher and higher until old timers along the river said they had never seen it so deep. Temperatures went down to 45 degrees and more below zero, and stayed there. For six weeks the thermometer never got above -32 degrees. One day a plane took off at Birches, on the Yukon at 72 degrees below. It had been claimed that motors wouldn't run when it was more than 40 degrees below, but the PIA kept schedule regardless of weather or of weather reports of "visibility nil."

Frozen noses, frozen knees, frozen toes were commonplace. The pilots and mechanics, while breaking planes loose when they were frozen down with the propellor blast in their faces, had their cheeks stiff half the time. Larry Davis frosted his lungs. Feet sweated in heavy fur mukluks in the heated cabins and then froze when the pilot or flight mechanic stood on the ice warming motors or mushing through snow to mail boxes.

Those nightmarish mail boxes! Each one meant a landing in soft snow to put in a single letter. Or, if the flag was up, to land to pick up a letter addressed, perhaps, to the nearest neighbor down the river, just so the plane would have to stop and the lonely trapper could have a visit.

Keeping a schedule was real work. It meant lighting the firepots at every stop to keep the motors warm and covering the motors with tent-like covers. The skis must be taxied onto round poles to keep them from freezing fast. A helper stood by with fire extinguisher in hand while the pilot mushed through the snow to the mail box or post office. If stops were of any length the oil must be drained, and many stops were more than 15 minutes by the time the pilot hiked to the post office and checked over the pouches with the postmaster. Some post offices were so far a dog team met the plane and took both pilot and mail to the post office.

Fred Milligan, a man who for nineteen years had driven dog team mail down the river, was hired as flight mechanic. Fred was openly antagonistic toward airplanes, but a few trips converted him into an ardent enthusiast and his knowledge of the river was invaluable. Later he spoke in disgust about "the long cold days put in on the trails down there, mushing dogs all day and getting as far as we can fly in 15 minutes."

Many postmasters still adhered to dog team ways. They disliked a wild pilot with a mail sack in one hand and a watch in the other, hurrying to conserve daylight. But soon most postmasters were glad to speed the mail and at the first sound of the motor began making up their pouches.

The pilots flew long hours. Al Monsen was in the air 90 hours in

December, when there were not more than 4 hours of light a day, and 102 hours in March. (The Department of Commerce disapproved of a pilot flying more than 80 hours a month). The Kusko Times of Takotna used to carry the item, "Al Monsen arrived with the mail and left immediately." It became a slogan for the pilots. They arrived with the mail and left immediately!

The telegraph lines gave a weather report every morning at 9 o'clock but the pilots seldom waited for this service. They flew as far as they could and if the weather got too thick they sat down and waited for it to lift a little. Joe once took three days to go to Tanana, only a hundred miles away, but the weather report was straight 'visibility nil' the whole three days.

Jinks commented mildly one evening that he wished it would clear up enough so that he could see what the opposite bank of the Yukon looked like. He had been up and down it with Lon for a month and hadn't seen across yet.

The Anchorage radio station reported that all planes there and at Fairbanks were grounded due to weather, but that same day three PIA planes left Nenana on their regular runs.

Selecting weather reports at random from the files I will copy a few representative ones, giving weather along the routes where schedules were maintained. These show the conditions under which the P.I.A. pioneered mail by air in Alaska.

"January 16, 1932:

Nulato, clear, visibility unlimited, temperature minus 51.
Kaltag, clear, unlimited, minus 50.
Unalakleet, clear, unlimited, minus 18.
(Note: that sudden rise in temperature across the coast mountains might mean danger of icing on the wings.)
Ruby, clear, unlimited, minus 46.
Flat, clear, unlimited, minus 40.
McGrath, clear, unlimited, minus 54.
Takotna, clear minus 45.
Fairbanks, dense ground fog, visibility nil, minus 46.
Hot Springs, dense ground fog, minus 55.
Tanana, dense ground fog, visibility nil, minus 58."

From the trip reports I find that on January 15 and 16 pilot Valley, flying the small chartered plane, flew from Nenana to Ruby, with stops at Hot Springs, Tanana, and with back stops at Kokrines, Mason's Slough, Tanana, Fish Lake, Hot Springs, Tolovana, and Nenana, carrying 519 pounds of mail and flying approximately 500 miles.

Between January 13 and 16 Alex Holden flew from Nenana to Unalakleet with stops at Tanana, Fish Lake, Ruby, Koyukuk and

Nulato, and back with stops at Kaltag, Nulato, Koyukuk, Galena, Ruby and Nenana, a total of 960 miles, carrying full loads of mail each way.

On January 16 Joe flew from Anchorage to Nenana, 300 miles, bringing up the Bellanca from an overhaul in the P.I.A. hangar down there.

Here's another weather report which would make a pilot want to turn over in bed and keep on sleeping.

January 30, 1932:

Nulato, foggy, visibility nil.

Unalakleet, overcast, nil.

Kaltag, light snow.

Ruby, overcast, 1000 foot visibility

Takotna, light snow.

McGrath, snowing.

Fairbanks, snow, visibility nil.

Hot Springs, overcast, 1500 foot visibility.

Tanana, snowing, visibility nil.

On January 29, Al Monsen started his regular Kuskokwim trip, completing it February 2nd, with stops at Lake Minchumina, Medfra, McGrath, Takotna, Ophir, Crooked Creek and Flat on the way out, and the same with the omission of Ophir and Crooked Creek on the way back. He flew 1140 miles with two passengers, 150 pounds of freight, and 1598 pounds of mail.

January 30, Joe flew to Minto, Tolovana, Dugan Creek, Hot Springs, Fish Lake, and Tanana. Returning, he was forced down by thick snow near Eight Mile Island and when the snow lifted he went on the Fish Lake, Hot Springs, Tolovana and in to Nenana. This was all in weather reported impossible for flying. He had the regular mail and 132 pounds of freight.

On February 11 and 12 there were more low temperatures, ranging from a *high* of -34° in Unalakleet to a low of 57° below zero at Tanana, and from clear weather to dense ground fog.

On February 11, 12, and 13 Lon Cope made the Yukon mail run. On February 12 Joe flew the way mail to Tanana carrying six passengers for different stops. He had 687 pounds of mail and flew 305 miles that day.

On February 11, Al Monsen completed his Kuskokwim trip to Bethel, making stops at Lake Minchumina, Medfra, McGrath, Takotna, Ophir, back to McGrath, on to Iditarod, Crooked Creek, Napiamute, Akiak, and Bethel. Returning, he added Sleitmute to the other stops. He left Nenana with 1057 pounds of mail, 300 pounds of freight, his flight mechanic, and the postal inspector, and flew a total of 1530 miles.

The next day, February 12, he flew from Nenana to Anchorage, picking up an Alaska Railroad employee who had frozen his hand and taking him to the Anchorage hospital for treatment. The weather was so bad that Al had to fly between the hills, following the railroad tracks. He said afterward that he folded back the Fairchild wings and flew through the tunnels, too!

"An account of this flight was written up in Rex Beach's article, "Flying Frontiersmen", which was published in the *American Magazine*, April, 1936. This same article also tells of Joe's salvage of the Fleetster from the lake near Telegraph Creek.

I have gone into detail with these reports because they were actually history in the making. They showed winter weather in the interior of Alaska. And they proved that neither extremely low temperatures nor unfavorable weather stopped the P.I.A. in the performance of schedules. At one time three P.I.A. planes landed and departed at Tanana while a passenger there waited for a plane from a rival company in Fairbanks.

For years Joe had been known in California as a pilot who could get through, no matter what the weather conditions.

Once in Los Angeles I got a wire that he was coming down from San Francisco and would land at six o'clock. I went out to the field and an attendant asked what I wanted. I said I was waiting for a plane.

"There won't be any planes in this evening," he said. "Visibility is nil, They're all grounded." Then, curiously, "Who were you expecting?"

"Joe Barrows, from Oakland."

"Oh!" he said. "Well, *he'll* be in."

Sure enough, at exactly six o'clock, I heard the Fairchild at the end of the runway and saw it taxi into sight through the fog.

When we first lived in Alameda, back in 1926, Joe was often called early in the morning to fly across the hills to Concord to guide the mail planes in over a Bay fog. That was long before radio or radar or other guides were used. All this time he was studying navigation and blind flying when other pilots were laughing at him, or becoming alarmed for fear his ideas might be put across and they would be forced to learn that sort of flying themselves. Which proved to be true!

The small Fairchild 51 and the Bellanca made the way stops where the larger Fairchilds could not get in and out. However, in March, when the snow's crust was harder, Al Monsen made the Yukon "RFD" line a few times with a Fairchild 71. The pilots not only flew, but they snowshoed runways, dug the planes out of deep snow, warmed the motors, and made personal contacts along the mail lines which built up confidence and friendships.

In February, still in the midst of 'deep cold', the postal

inspector, Mr. Marchand, rode the mail lines and saw for himself the job the P.I.A. had been up against and how they had fulfilled His praise was unrestrained.

I sent for mail-order snowsuits for Teddy and Margie Lou. Lon took measurements of our feet, drawn on wrapping paper, and a Lapp lady in Unalakleet made fur mukluks for us. Margie's and Teddy's were little ankle-length fur boots with gay checkered fur trimming and bright tassels. Mine were knee-high, the most comfortable foot gear I had ever worn. In February Joe bought me a muskrat fur coat in Fairbanks, my first fur coat. I had been wearing a light polo coat all winter. Now we were all dressed for the northland.

In the fall I had frozen my knees in Fairbanks when I foolishly walked eleven blocks to a bridge party at 30° below, wearing silk stockings. I found that the other women had worn mukluks, or woolen stockings and tights which they 'checked' when they arrived. After that my knees frosted easily. I also froze my nose one night in Nenana when we all walked out to the mission to a party. It was way below zero and the walk was a good long mile. As I opened the door and stepped inside the mission building a man greeted my saying,

"Pardon me, madam, but your nose is frozen."

Lon rubbed the whitened member with snow and for the rest of the evening it glowed like Rudolph's. Margie Lou's cheekbones seemed most susceptible and many times I saw them turning white in two little spots and rushed her to the nearest snowbank. But in March as the weather warmed up a little I turned Margie Lou and Teddy out to play in their snowsuits, mukluks, mittens, and caps, with scarves tied around their necks.

With spring and another mining season at hand business began to pour in, more than four planes could handle. Incoming loads of fur filled the planes, sent as parcel post to Seattle. Our contracts weren't for air mail, remember. They were regular star route contracts so we carried letters, newspapers, magazines, parcel post, everything went by air at regular postal rates. Often planes came in with the flight mechanic stretched out on top of sacks of fur with the pilot even holding a sack on his lap. Orders were placed for freight, cases of eggs, fresh meat, perishables. And as the trails began to thaw the prospectors along the rivers used the planes to fly between villages.

On one trip Joe came in with a traveling dentist aboard, and his dental chair and three dogs.

"And the darned dogs were air sick, too," exclaimed Fred Milligan in disgust.

An extra plane and pilot from Fairbanks were hired to help

finish the mail, letting Lon Cope go to Anchorage to make preparations for summer business.

In March we received a large freight order from Tom Devane at Ruby, an order to haul fourteen thousand pounds of freight to a mine sixty miles back in the hills, where of course no roads existed.

April brought the impending break-up of the river ice. We sighed with relief as each trip was checked off. After break-up the river boats would carry the mail.

Nenana was buzzing with the excitement of the Annual Ice Pool. All Alaska made guesses about what day, hour and minute the ice will move in the Tanana River below the railroad bridge. Tickets with the estimated time on them cost one dollar apiece and the stubs were deposited in cans in every village. That year the pool was sixty thousand dollars. We bought ten tickets and placed them in a sealed can. On April 12th the ticket sale closed all over the territory and the cans were brought to Nenana where the tickets were sorted, tabulated, and listed according to days, hours and minutes. The finished lists made a book as large as a city telephone directory.

On a hunch I bought a ticket for 9:15 on the morning of May first. The ice went out on May first all right, but at 10:15, just an hour later. My hunch must have been in the wrong time zone. And there went my sixty thousand dollars.

Al Monsen flew to the Kuskokwim with the last load of mail. Single-handed, he had maintained an unbroken schedule since January first and he was as proud as if he had dug the Panama Canal unaided.

"Joe, we did it," he boasted. "They all told us up and down the rivers that it couldn't be done. But we've showed 'em."

Applause greeted our pilots all along the line. The former enemies, the old dog team men, had received their mail ten days to a month faster and their furs were on the Seattle market three weeks earlier. They had also ordered eggs and oranges and other perishables all winter, luxuries hitherto unavailable after freeze-up. The railroad was now only a few hours away instead of twenty dog team days.

The contracts were ended. The record was made. The P.I.A. had carried star route mail in one of Alaska's worst winters. If it could be done with poor, inadequate equipment and without servicing facilities, how much more easily could it be done with proper backing, with hangars and spare motors.

Joe flew to Seward and caught a ship for Seattle enroute to New York to try to sell the company, this time with something definite to sell—mail contracts, a profitable freight and passenger business, and the finest personnel anywhere.

Lon Cope reported that the apartment we rented the year before in Anchorage was again available, so the children and I went back there, waiting to find out what our next move was to be.

The first night I woke up every time a car went past. I wasn't used to the noises of a city!

CHAPTER TEN

My Solo Flight

It was a lovely warm day in the middle of June, 1932. The children and I left the hospital and walked slowly up the hill toward Anchorage's business section. I wasn't conscious of walking—rather I floated on air, for I was extremely happy.

I had just taken a physical examination and had been given a student permit allowing me to take flying lessons.

Dr. Romig, back there in the old railroad hospital, had put me through a whole series of tests. I had closed my eyes and stood on one leg to see if my sense of balance was all right. I sat quietly while he listened to my heart and took my blood pressure. Then I sat at one end of a room and pulled little strings to align bolts in a box seemingly a quarter of a mile away. This was a depth perception test and the one I feared most as I wasn't sure just how good my eyes really were.

"Well, you passed for a private license," Dr. Romig's kindly old face beamed at me as he ran his hand through his shock of gray hair. "Your eyes aren't good enough so that you could ever get a transport license unless they should improve. But you passed all the tests for a private license. Now go on and learn to fly—but be careful."

I assured him I had no intention of trying for a transport license.

Big and distinguished looking, Dr. Romig was one of Alaska's leading doctors who had spent years of pioneering in the north. He had lived at Bethel at the Moravian Mission there and by many outstanding exploits of the early days had earned the title of 'The Dog Team Doctor'. Since then a book has been written about him, using that title.

For eight years I had wanted to fly, since I took my first ride in the cow pasture in San Jacinto. I had never been physically active, had not cared for athletics. But I had always wanted equal rights with my brothers—it hadn't seemed fair that boys got to do all the exciting things.

When I was sixteen Violet and I finally won our parent's grudging consent to allow us to make a 300 mile horseback trip from Ashland to my uncle's ranch on the coast and back. We promised to stay in hotels overnight, but could cook our meals out. We wore six-shooters at our belts and carried cartridges in case it became necessary to defend our honor. The occasion never arose. But not until Violet's long riding skirt nearly hung her from the saddle horn were we allowed to wear breeches. Girls in pants just weren't ladylike. That eight day horseback trip was the talk of the town. The paper printed a news item, calling us 'intrepid damsels'. Then and there I decided to go on being intrepid, seeking adventures. And I had married an aviator.

I had no desire to engage in aviation commercially. I didn't want to fly the mail or pilot a transport plane. I just wanted to prove that I could learn, what Amelia Earhart once called a 'woman's reason'. Men were such superior creatures, no matter how modern they thought they were. Most of them believed that *any* man could drive a car better than *all* women. Pilots stood around the field when a woman took off as if they considered every flight a potential crack-up. One of our pilots once congratulated me when he saw me make a good landing, saying,

"Why, Mary, that was great. You came in and landed just like anybody!" He meant, of course, that I had surprisingly landed just as well as a man could have done.

Remember, this was 1932, when there was still controversy about women trying to mix marriages and careers. The concensus was that she could have one or the other, but not both.

When I asked Joe if I might learn to fly (for after all he earned the money which would pay for any lessons) his tone was one of amused indulgence.

"You can't learn to fly. You get airsick too easily." And then, adding insult to injury he continued, "but I'll let you hold the stick sometimes when we are in the air."

I didn't want to just hold the stick, I wanted to fly by myself. And now, with a student permit in my pocket, I was ready to begin. Joe was in New York and wouldn't hear about it, or be worried until I let him know that I had soloed. I would surprise him.

Three young men had recently come to Anchorage and started a flying school at Merrill Field. They had a Fleet biplane in which to give instruction. These men were Steve Mills, Jack Waterworth, and Charles Ruttan. Already they had a dozen or more students.

I bought myself a pair of jodhjur breeches and a blazer jacket made from a Hudson's Bay blanket. Lon Cope loaned me one of his old helmets and I was all equipped to learn to fly.

Merrill Field, named for an early day pilot, Russell Merrill, was about a mile from town, along a lovely country road, bordered in June with delicate pink wild roses and masses of flaming purple fireweed. Teddy and Margie Lou walked out with me every fine morning and sat on an empty gasoline case while I took my twenty minutes of dual instruction time.

The air work came easily and I felt that I was making immense strides. Then I began practicing landings and take-offs. The more I learned about the operation of the plane, about its feel in the air, the more interested I became. Why, this was one of the most exciting things I had ever done. I tried to hold the plane straight down the runway as we took off, made a climbing turn, and throttled back to fly around the airport until I was in position to glide down for a landing. Down, down toward the brush at the end of the field—was I too high, or was I high enough to clear it? Then the wheels settled down on the runway and I had a feeling of immense pride.

Some days I felt that I was learning rapidly. I was master of the plane and it obeyed my commands. Other days were a constant battle with controls and perverse winds and air pockets. Then the plane took the bit in its teeth, so to speak and, no matter how tightly I clung to the stick, I had a feeling that its racing horse-power was mocking me—that I would never be able to subdue it.

Lon and Margaret Cope came out one Sunday afternoon to watch me, and I groundlooped on the take-off and headed straight for the hangar. Steve grabbed the controls for I, panic-stricken, hadn't the faintest idea what to do. At times like that I was afraid of the power of the throbbing engine. Accidents could happen so quickly. As Eyore, in "Winnie the Pooh", said, "Accidents are funny things. You never know you're having one until you have it."

Gradually I piled up seven hours of instruction time. I was a little ashamed of this. My brother, Frank, had soloed in a little over four hours, and Jinks Ames, one of our mechanics, had soloed after only an hour and twenty minutes of dual. I told myself that Jinks had an advantage as he had been flying with Lon every day all winter and must have absorbed the feel of the plane by osmosis. I also rationalized that I must be very sure of myself before I jeopardized my life so that I wouldn't leave two motherless children.

One hot July evening I had a particularly bad session. The air was dead. Dust hung over the field from my take off until I landed. As I came down into it the horizon was blotted out and I groundlooped into the brush beside the runway. The mechanics came to pull the plane back onto the grass and I longed to hide away in some very small hole. To diminish me further another student, a German, who was good and knew that he was good, came up to me and said,

"Too bad, but women aren't supposed to fly anyway. A woman's place is in the home."

At that moment I was half inclined to agree. Perhaps I was too ambitious, attempting something for which the Lord hadn't intended me—or He would have given me wings. Here was I, a mother of two small children, risking my neck in so foolhardy a fashion. Had I any right to take such chances? That evening I was so discouraged I almost quit.

But the next morning, the twenty-seventh of July, was a clear, windy one and when Steve phoned that he would pick me up I hurried into my breeches and jacket and determined to try again.

I climbed into the rear cockpit of the Fleet and buckled on my helmet which had speaking tubes attached through which the instructor in the front cockpit could deliver directions and comments. This is a beastly device for a woman for there is no provision for talking back! Steve got in front and fastened his safety belt. I taxied onto the field, swung into the runway and took off straight into the wind, made a circle of the field, and came in for a beautiful landing. The breeze was stiff, but it helped me to hold the plane steady.

"Make two more rounds as good as that and I'll let you solo," came Steve's voice through the speaking tube.

So around the field I went again. The air was rough and it required my constant attention to keep the plane steady, but it helped in landing. When I slowed down after the second round Steve unbuckled his safety belt and turned around.

"Want to solo?" he asked.

Now that the moment had actually come I was lacking in self-confidence.

"Do you think I can?" I wanted assurance, but he didn't give it to me.

"Do *you* think you can?" he countered.

"I can try," I replied.

Steve climbed out of the plane. He tied his handerchief to a wing strut. That white streamer let the flying world know that a novice was trying the air on wobbly wings. As I saw the trailing white banner I began to realize what I was about to do.

Then Steve stepped back.

"All right. You can do it. Go ahead."

I didn't hesitate, but opened the throttle and went down the field. The tail came up. I was in the air. It had been a good take-off. And not until that minute did the realization come to me that I was up—up in the air all alone. The front cockpit loomed big and empty without Steve's familiar head and shoulders up there. The plane seemed lighter without his weight; I thought it bounced more in the freshening wind.

The engine throbbed with power as I banked and made a climbing turn. Could I manage it all myself, without Steve's hand up there on the dual control in case of emergency or errors of judgment? The throttle was pulled back to flying speed and I took a moment to look down at the field.

The mechanics had all gathered in front of the hangar as they always did to watch a solo—probably wanting to miss nothing if the student should crack up. I saw Steve and Jack Waterworth standing a little apart, probably praying while their only airplane was in such unskilled hands. A crack-up would wash out their flying school! Then I saw the tiny figures which were Margie Lou and Teddy, their faces turned upward toward their mother in the sky above them.

Again I looked about me. Mount McKinley was visible, dominating the skyline of the Alaska Range to the north. The Susitna wound down from its sides to the head of Cook Inlet, whose waters were blue in the sun. Anchorage streets were neatly laid out in checkerboard patterns with tiny houses in each square. An engine puffed down on the Alaska Railroad tracks. Purple fireweed banked the fence corners.

One of our mechanics had soloed a few nights before and had overshot the field so that he had to go around and try again before he could land. I must do better than that! I must make a good landing. But how I dreaded to start down; I was safe as long as I stayed in the air. I remembered a student Joe told about once who had stayed up, flying round and round, afraid to come down, until he ran out of gas.

Suddenly I found that I was praying, repeating over and over the words, "The Lord will preserve me from evil."

My nervousness left me. My hand on the stick was steady, my brain was giving orders clearly. I circled over a patch of burned trees, over a little farm house. These were my landmarks. Now it was time to square away with the field. Now it was time to cut the switch.

Down, down toward the field. I was a little high after all as I came over the edge of the brush to the runway. I touched the ground. The plane bounced. For a fleeting second I panicked. Was it a high bounce? Should I give the motor the gun and go on up again? No, the plane settled down onto the runway. I held the stick back firmly against my stomach and clamped on left rudder to counteract a ground loop. Then gently I applied both brakes. The Fleet slowed to a stop. I kicked it around, opened the throttle slightly and taxied up in front of the hangar. With one motion I cut the gas and the switch and then sank back, breathing a great sigh of relief.

It was over. I was safely down.

Jinks and Larry and Loren and the other mechanics ran out,

crowding around to congratulate me. Margie Lou climbed up against the cockpit.

"Mother, that was fine. I'm so proud of you." Her wide grin showed two missing front teeth.

Teddy looked me over, interested, and yet half doubting.

"Can you weally fly by yourself, muvver? Can you weally, all by yourself?"

I took off my helmet and found that my forehead was wet with perspiration. I unfastened my safety belt with suddenly clammy fingers and, as I climbed out of the cockpit, I realized that my heart was pounding and my knees were rubbery. Reaction had set in and I was more nervous than I had been in the actual flight.

Back in town, as the noon whistles began to blow, I wired Joe in New York.

"Soloed safely this morning."

The wire cost $3.65.

It was evening of the next day before I went to the field again. The apartment house had just had new Flamo stoves installed, and I had enjoyed cooking a big meal after struggling with the little kerosene range we had formerly. I remember that I made buttermilk biscuits for our dinner and baked a fluffy salmon souffle and some potatoes. It was fun to have a reliable oven again. It was late when I finished the dishes, but the evenings in July were still long and bright.

The wind had changed and I had to use the long runway. It just happened that I had not made many landings and take-offs from it and I was not as familiar with the approaches, nor as sure of myself.

"Do you want to solo tonight?" Jack Waterworth, who was my instructor this evening, turned around to ask.

I found that I was dreading a second solo. I had done it once, but it might have been a lucky accident. Maybe I shouldn't push my luck.

"No, I don't think I better," I shook my head.

But Jack probably realized that the longer I put it off the harder it would be for me to nerve myself to do it, so he climbed out in a very determined way.

"Go ahead." It was an order, and I obeyed.

After that second solo I began to have confidence in myself and every good day after that I went to the field and piled up solo minutes. Then I practiced figure eights and spirals and spot landings so that I could try for my private license when the Department of Commerce Inspector came to Alaska in September on his semi-annual round. At that time it was possible to earn a private license with only ten hours of solo time. The following year,

I think it was, the requirement was raised to fifty hours.

My log book recorded just twelve hours of solo time when the Inspector arrived, but I expected him to be in town at least two weeks so that I could build up a little more experience before I attempted the flight tests. The evening after he arrived all of us students were called together in the P.I.A. offices for our written tests on Air Commerce Rules and Regulations. I had studied so this was not hard.

The next morning about eleven o'clock Steve phoned me.

"I want you to come right out and take your examination."

My heart stopped. I hadn't been expecting to take it until the last minute before the inspector left. But with shaking hands I crawled into my sweater and breeches and when Steve drove up to the apartment house I was ready to go with him.

The inspector, Jim Peyton, was standing by the hangar doors. There was an air of solemnity all around. Steve and Jack looked serious—after all we were their students. All eleven or twelve of the students were there, waiting for their turns, and each looked a little more frightened than the last. I was the only woman.

"He's being pretty tough," one of the students whispered to me. "Asking us to do vertical banks and so on—a regular Limited Commercial test."

I was more nervous than I had ever been in my life as I watched Bob Carlson, a young high school student, come in for a good landing. The inspector passed him, and I watched as he wrote out a Letter of Authority.

Then it was my turn. I climbed into the plane, listened while Mr. Peyton gave me instructions about making figure eight turns, and directions about making a spiral down from two thousand feet to a spot landing directly in front of McGee's hangar. I fastened down my helmet and buckled my safety belt, pulled the goggles down over my eyes, and was off. Those figure eights almost got me—vertical banks without gaining or losing altitude were no cinch for a student with twelve hours of solo! Then I climbed up to two thousand feet, shut off the motor, made three 360 degree turns, and at last brought the wheels down to the airport for a spot landing.

How relieved I was when it was over, and how incredulous I felt when the inspector got out a pencil, rested his pad on his knee, and wrote me out a Letter of Authority. I had passed! I was a licensed pilot!

Holding the precious paper proudly, I went into the hangar and there I found out why Steve had hurried me out to the field. The first three applicants who had tried for their tests had all failed. Among them was our star student, the blustering German who had thirty-five hours of solo time and was really good. But in the test he developed 'buck fever' or something and flubbed it. Steve had felt that if I heard about the failures I would get nervous so he wanted me to take my test before I knew of the slaughter which had gone before me.

Only Bob Carlson and I passed that day. Later a dentist and a mining man passed. When the inspector went on the Fairbanks there was sadness behind him because only four of twelve students had passed—and I was the only woman who had gone up for a license.

As far as I know, I was the first woman who took all of her training and received her license in Alaska.

CHAPTER ELEVEN

Up in the Air

September in Alaska is the loveliest month of the year. Other months in other places have their points—March in Berkeley with pink flowering trees in bloom, April in the Northwest with the daffodils and tulips blossoming and the dogwood white against the green of the evergreens, summers in the Oregon pine woods when mornings are just crisp enough for a wood fire or summers along the coast lying in the sun-baked sand while the breakers roll in.

But in September I would like to be in Alaska when the wild ducks fly overhead bound for California rice marshes, and the birch trees change overnight to bright gold, when the cranberry brush is red and blueberries are ripe and there is a hint of frost in the air. The hills turn into massy Persian rugs of golds, scarlets, greens and browns, with blue rivers threaded between. Lands which never have frosts miss the beauty of autumn foliage.

Alaskan birches are beautiful any time of the year, beautiful with their stark bare trunks against the snow and their equally stark shadows under the winter moon. In spring their tender young leaves are a delicate green, and in summer they weave lacy patterns of shade and sunshine, but in autumn they are breath-takingly lovely in their golden glory. Even I, (and no one is less talented, bought a box of crayons and tried to sketch a birch tree. Oh, to be an artist!

After the first frost the mosquitoes are gone and it is a delight to walk the trails out through the cranberry brush. The children and I gathered berries for jelly and jam.

Margie Lou was six so I took her to the school offices. The principal called the first and second grade teachers and asked her to read aloud to them. Fluently and with good expression she read in both first and second readers. She showed them an example of her handwriting and they agreed to let her try work in the second grade.

Reluctantly, Teddy went off to kindergarten, loitering all the way, feeling that the only good thing about being cooped up for a few hours was that it freed him from being required to take an afternoon nap.

I sent up to Fairbanks for our dishes and radio. We were comfortable in the apartment, but it wasn't a home.

After visiting a friend, I drew up house plans and worked out a simple rectangle with living room, dining room and kitchen on one side, three bedrooms and bathroom on the other. An Anchorage contractor estimated that he could build such a house for us at a cost of about $3000. What would it cost in Anchorage today?

Making house plans was really only wishful thinking. We didn't know where we would be the next year, or even the next month. I even tried writing a poem, one verse going something like this:

All I want is a little house
In a quiet, tree-shaded town,
Where Hubby will stop his roving
And say, "Here we'll settle down."

At last we received word that the P.I.A. had been sold to Pan-American Airways. The big company was also buying the Alaskan Airways, a Fairbanks-based operation. This sale probably began when Joe met Colonel Lindbergh in Nome the year before and seemed to indicate that Pan-Am was considering a route to the Orient.

Toward the end of October the last papers were signed and we got a check for our back wages. None of the pilots or mechanics had been paid in full for more than a year. We had taken money in bits and dribbles to pay rent and buy groceries. Now here was a check for nearly $3,000. That would build a house. That would buy us a home.

It was November before Joe came back to Alaska. We hadn't seen him since May. He was in charge of ferrying three Fairchild airplanes from New York to Fairbanks. I flew up with Al Monsen to meet him on a cloudless day, with a wing-strut thermometer registering 40 degrees below zero. Mt. McKinley was white against the skyline.

Joe's first news was disheartening. A physical examination had found spots on his lungs and the doctor said he must go to a warm climate. Accordingly, Pan American was sending him to Miami, Florida to take training on the airlines out of there.

I begged to go along, taking the children. The winter sunshine would also be good for them. But it was too expensive for all of us to go for just a few months.

We had Thanksgiving in Anchorage, the family together for the first time in six months. Then Joe flew back to Fairbanks and I began packing. We didn't know whether we would come back to Alaska or not, but it would be cheaper for me to stay somewhere 'Outside' on the west coast until we found where Joe was to be stationed next. Our dishes and radio went back to Fairbanks, in storage. When would I ever see, or use, my things again I wondered.

Margaret and Lon Cope were also packing. Lon was being sent to Brownsville, Texas to begin co-piloting the airliners over Mexico and Central America. He surely deserved the best, for he was one of Alaska's aviation pioneers, and certainly one of the finest, most loyal men who ever lived. Everyone envied him the opportunity to fly tri-motored, radio-equipped planes after shepherding the old Fairchilds over the Alaskan tundra.

With only our suitcases and one trunk containing clothing and necessary linens, we boarded the train on December 2nd, 1932. Joe had boarded in Fairbanks and we continued to Seward to meet an Alaska Steamship liner for Seattle. I looked back at the snowy streets of Anchorage as the train pulled out, waving goodbye to the friends who had come to the depot to see us off.

Joe was ill. His future was uncertain. If he passed his next physical after his training in Miami he might be sent back to Alaska, or he might go to any other of the Pan-Am divisions. In the meantime the family was apart again. I must find another furnished apartment and get Margie Lou back in school, waiting until he had a definite assignment. I was very depressed. We were more unsettled than we had been since we first went to Alaska.

Eight days later we arrived in Seattle, in rain instead of snow. And two days after that Joe took a train eastbound. It was ten months before the children saw him again. He promised to let us know as soon as possible where we were to go. In the meantime I was to stay in an apartment hotel in downtown Seattle, waiting.

Any mother who ever spent two weeks in a hotel with small children knows how difficult it is to entertain them and keep them quiet. They climbed the stairs, they ran the service elevator. We walked the streets until we were all exhausted.

Christmas came and we still had no definite directive from Joe. On my own I stored the trunk and we took a bus up to Bellingham to spend the holidays with my cousin in the beautiful little Dutch town of Lynden.

An air mail letter arrived saying that Joe would be in New York another week. Then to Miami for a few weeks and on to Brownsville where he might remain two months. We might be able to come to Texas, but in the meantime to stay where we were.

I rented a three room apartment in Lynden and had our trunk sent up. We had a living room, kitchen, bedroom, bath, a private entrance, electric stove, steam heat, all for $25 a month. Margie Lou started to the Lynden grade school, her second school and second teacher during her first year of school.

These were still deep depression days. Prices were cheap. I stocked up with groceries at the Lynden Department Store. Thinking in terms of Alaskan prices I ordered a dollar's worth of potatoes and a quarter's worth of carrots. I got a 100 pound sack of potatoes and a huge bag of carrots. Milk at the door was 11¢ a quart, just raised from 9¢. In Alaska we had paid 25¢. At a nearby creamery I could get a bottle of buttermilk for a nickel, and down the street was a Dutch bakery where fresh bread came from the ovens about eleven o'clock in the morning.

In January Joe wired asking if I could come to Brownsville, without the children, to take a trip with him over the Pan American Airlines through Central America. My cousins, Marion and Dick, said they would take care of the children. So I gave up the apartment, put my trunk in their basement, left the children, and on a snowy winter evening Dick drove me to Bellingham to catch a south-bound bus. I wore my fur coat because it was so cold. We had to stop to wipe snow from the windshield as we drove.

From Seattle I went by train, being reminded of the Alaskan Railroad near Broad Pass as we went through high snow banks in the Cascades. I spent a day in Oakland with sister Edith and my brother Frank and my sister-in-law, Marjorie. I spent another day in Los Angeles with Dad and Mother Barrows. Mother had prepared my favorite foods for dinner and I remember how good an artichoke tasted. We didn't get artichokes in Alaska! Then I went east on the Overland Limited, taking a side trip out of Phoenix to view ancient cliff dwellings. Joe met me at the Brownsville depot and took me to have breakfast with Margaret Cope. Her baby son was just three weeks old, Edward—nick-named Teddy.

Brownsville was delightful in February with orange blossoms perfuming the air. It was warm enough to go coatless. I certainly didn't need my fur coat. We stayed at the El Jardin Hotel for three weeks. During that time I did a lot of typing for Joe, studied Spanish, and went to the airport to fly a time or two in a funny little Curtiss-Wright pusher which seemed more like a glider than an airplane.

In the evenings we went across the bridge with the Copes, or some of the Pan-Am group, to have dinner at Matamores. In the little cafes we could get two kinds of meat, one perhaps wild game such as venison or duck, a salad, tortillas, and all the trimmings for 50¢. Afterward we danced to Mexican music or walked the streets of the quiet little town watching the people as they promenaded around the square, men walking in one direction and the women in the other. There were interesting little shops in which to browse and we enjoyed the uncommercialized atmosphere.

At last Joe was ready to take the tour of the airlines to the south. He was in training for an executive position and needed to study the details of Pan American's operations.

CHAPTER TWELVE

Caribbean Cruise

On February 24th we flew from Brownsville in a tri-motored Ford, bound for Mexico City. A crew of four, pilot, co-pilot, radio operator and steward were all dressed in neat uniforms. The young Mexican steward brought us Spanish magazines, gum to chew, and cotton for our ears. He provided pillows to tuck behind our heads if we wished to nap. Our seats were comfortable, adjustable, with spotless linen covers. There was even a lavatory in the plane's rear. Such comfort was unbelievable.

South across the Rio Grande, over the Gulf of Mexico where breakers lace-edged the shore below. Down over jungle trees, palm-thatched huts to our first landing at the outskirts of Tampico. Oil tankers lay at anchor in the harbor.

We entered a pleasant, flower-bordered station with a shaded passageway to the building. This station was typical of the Pan American stations along the way. All were attractive and all were clean—cleanliness was stressed. There was a restaurant where we ate sandwiches while waiting for our next plane, a tri-motored Fokker of the Aerovias Centrales.

Over mountains and valleys to Mexico City. The pilot detoured to circle over the ancient pyramids of San Juan Teotihuacan before landing at the 7000 foot elevation of Mexico City's plateau, only five flying hours from Brownsville.

Our three days in Mexico City were memorable, but only a tantalizer to lure us back. It is a city where old and new rub elbows comfortably. I had not realized Mexico City was so old. There was a University established here before the Pilgrim Fathers landed on Plymouth Rock. Beside modernistic buildings were ancient cathedrals with pink lava rock walls, and Indian markets with women squatting beside piles of tomatoes, peppers, and chilis, or men with pottery and baskets for sale.

On Sunday we drove to the floating gardens of Xochomilco and rented a boat to mingle with merry-makers, swimmers, vegetable and flower-laden dugout canoes. On the banks Indian women pounded clothes on stones to wash them. We could have hired a boatload of musicians to serenade us as we floated on the placid waters. The gardens dated to pre-conquest times.

The Mexican food was wonderful. I remember a dinner at the old San Angel Inn near Cortez's palace where we ate in what was once a convent garden. We had breakfast at Sanborn's (where Joe met an aviator friend from Detroit), lunch at Paolo's and dinner at Prendes'. When we tried our faltering Spanish on the waiter, he usually asked us in good English what we wanted.

Sunday afternoon we attended a bull fight where a visiting matador from Spain gave an exhibition, ending when the bull whirled and gored him the leg so badly that he died that night. I'm not sure I'm glad I saw a bullfight, but it certainly was colorful. The immense stands were full of brightly dressed women and handsome, dark-eyed men. The picadors wore gay silk blouses and rode blindfolded old horses. The toreadors wore bright yellows, pinks and lavendars and carried be-ribboned darts. Last came the matador with his scarlet cape.

My sympathies were with the horses and the bulls. The blindfolded horses were padded for protection but the padding ripped under prodding horns. And the bull's fight was sure to be a losing one. On bull, kindred of Ferdinand, refused to fight. Perhaps he too wanted to sit quietly and smell the flowers. The crowd began to boo and in a mass rose and turned their backs, refusing to look until he was taken away and replaced with a more aggressive bull.

Along dusty roads we went to the pyramids of the Sun and the Moon and I stood before these huge piles in open-mouthed amazement. In the Aztec sacrificial temple I shuddered to picture the human victims once sacrificed on the altar. The gargoyles on the newly excavated temples looked Oriental. How fascinating it would be to study archeology.

In the Shrine of Guadeloupe hung the painting of the Virgin Mary which appeared miraculously on the robe of an Indian. Penitents crawled along the streets and up the steps toward the altar. Nearly three miles away, on the dusty road, a woman crawled on her knees toward the church. Another woman walked beside her, holding an umbrella to shade the creeping penitent from the glaring sun.

Roads were bordered with maguey plants from which tequila and fiery pulque is made. On one 'pulqueria' was a sign reading 'get drunk here for ten centavos'. In a field ox teams pulled crude plows. Burros loaded with firewood plodded along.

Between sightseeing trips Joe and I explored the markets, leather shops, silver shops, or just walked along the streets. One morning I stood long before the huge mural on the walls of the Palace of Education, a grand scale painting by Diego Riveira depicting the history of Mexico.

Never were three days packed so full, with so much to be left to 'next time'.

Before dawn we rode through streets deserted save for here and there a lone woman kneeling by a tiny fire cooking tortillas for morning trade. As sunrise colors streaked the sky we took off, over the dry lake bed Carranza drained in the hope of finding Montezuma's hidden gold. The sun gilded the slopes of Mount Popocatapetl and the snowy outline of the Sleeping Lady and they glowed pink and orange above the shadow-filled valleys. Their names had fascinated me since I first read them in my brown geography book back in my one-room school on the Colorado prairie.

A landing at Tejaria, a junction for Vera Cruz, in moist warm sunshine at another flower-bordered station. Inside was a tiled floor, an attractive pictorial map on the wall, and most attractive of all, a food counter where we ordered breakfast. Mine was a Spanish omelette. Later we learned that the smiling Chinese cook had recently carved up another cook who had been sent to relieve him.

A young woman fellow-passenger had an English vocabulary as limited as my Spanish one but we conveyed meanings by signs and smiles and a few words. She was going to Costa Rica to be married. Our other passengers were a man bound for Lima and a New York doctor, a native Nicauraguan, going home for a vacation.

While we ate a tri-motor for Merida slipped in for a landing. Then one bell sounded and the flight crew marched to the plane. Two bells and we passengers went along the passageway, down a roped-off enclosure and boarded. Here at the jungle's edge, system was precise. This system, these spotless terminals, the well-kept planes, all inspired confidence in an airline which covered on schedule so much rugged country, and with such a high rating of safety.

While we flew over jungle the radio operator sat by his instruments, often handing messages to the pilots whose shoulders were seen up forward in a separate compartment. Joe read and I attempted, with my pocket Spanish-English dictionary, to decipher jokes in a Spanish magazine. Now and then I was able to get the point.

Scudding clouds, like whipped meringue, enveloped us before we dropped down over jungle growth to Tapachula. Immigrations officers checked our passports and baggage since we were now leaving Mexico. The air was tropical, moist and steamy. A young English woman with a tanned son in a meager playsuit watched us land. She borrowed American cigarettes from the flight crew and told us she lived on a coffee finca back in the hills. Tapachula had about 16,000 population she said, and she wished a revolution

Lon and Margaret Cope with mechanics Jinx Ames and Loren Fernald. Nenana

Al Monsen, Joe Barrows and Percy Hubbard. Nenana

*PIA planes on the river ice, makeshift shelter
in rear. Tanana River bridge in background*

Percy Hubbard delivering the rural free delivery mail

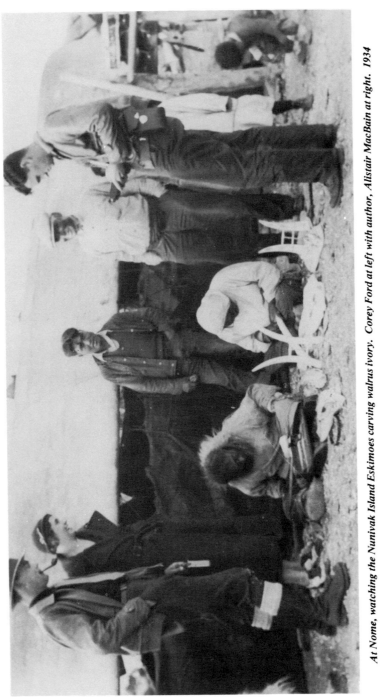

At Nome, watching the Nunivak Island Eskimoes carving walrus ivory. Corey Ford at left with author, Alistair MacBain at right. 1934

Routine freight load to interior, on ice at Ruby

Author with Steve Mills,
her instructor. Anchorage, 1932

After a successful
solo flight, Anchorage, 1932

First woman pilot trained and licensed in Alaska. 1932

Pan-American's Alaska employees, 1936

Front row, pilots in uniform, left to right: Al Monsen, Bill Knox, Joe Crosson, Joe Barrows, Walter Hall, Jerry Jones.   Photo taken in Fairbanks.

FLYING FAMILY

Although they some times get lonesome when their daddy, W. J. Barrows, pilot with the Pan-American Airways, is busy flying over South American, 8-year-old Margie and Lou and 6-year-old Teddy, as well as their pretty mother, an accomplished flyer herself, are are proud that they belong to a "flying family."
(For details see Page 2.)

Job of Flyer's Wife Holds Adventure—Lonesomeness

(See Page 1 for Photograph.)

If you're one of these women with a desire for a permanent hearth, at which to keep the home fires burning, and a husband who's always right there when you want him, don't marry a flyer.

That is the advice of Mrs. W. J Barrows, wife of a Pan-American Airways pilot, visiting at the Spring Apartment Hotel here with her two children, 8-year-old Margie Lou, and 6-year-old Teddy, while her husband is in Miami, Fla., preparing to take three planes to Fairbanks, Alaska.

But if you like variety, which, after all, is the spice of life, and adventure galore, an aviator is just the man for you, she quickly adds.

Farther North Each Time

"I've been married nine years and I've lived everywhere from San Diego, Calif., to Fairbanks, getting farther north every move," said Mrs. Barrows. She is slim and pretty, with large, expressive dark eyes. "I've had my furniture in storage for the past two years, and now I don't know when I'll be able to get it out.

"But there are so many compensations that I don't mind those little drawbacks. Last year I made a trip with my husband over the Pan-American Air Lines, flying over the Caribbean Sea and to South America. It was wonderful. Not many wives have an adventure like that."

She Is Pilot, Too

And Mrs. Barrows knows whereof she speaks, when she discusses aviation, for she is Alaska's only woman to win a pilot's license.

"I believe more and more women will be taking up flying as time goes on," she said, "but they will never be able to be transport pilots. The men won't let them. And they'll find they won't be able to overcome the male superiority complex."

Mrs. Barrows added that she and her husband intend to teach the children to fly when they are 16 years old.

"We come from a flying family," she said. "My brother, Frank Moore, is an aviator with the California Forest Service and my brother-in-law, Robert Barrows, is with the United Airlines in Oakland. And Margie had her first ride in San Diego when she was 5 months old."

Seattle Times—August 14, 1933

Joe and Al Monsen on Harding Lake at completion of their flight across northern Canada to Fairbanks

might come along to liven things up. Perhaps she was bored with life on a lonely plantation in a foreign land.

Over Guatemala the scenery was even lovelier, and it had all been lovely. Coffee fincas with clusters of red-roofed, white-walled buildings were set amidst green vegetation. Plants marched in even rows up and down the steep hills. In canyons silvery waterfalls dripped into emerald pools. All about crowded the jungle. Frequently an orange or scarlet flowering tree stood out against the green.

Guatemala City looked modern in the midst of a cultivated valley. I had hoped we were stopping over, but we only landed briefly. (Over forty years later I spent a week in this fascinating country.)

Airport attendants loaded the plane with exquisite flowers. Three beautiful black-eyed girls came aboard. One was a bride for whom the flowers were consigned. She was a daughter of a wealthy family, our doctor companion informed us, and her wedding had just been a social event. The newlyweds were bound for a honeymoon in Salvador. Guatemala is noted for its lovely women, and these examples helped prove the country's reputation.

Box lunches were served in the air, with paper cups of hot coffee. Still in the future were stewardesses serving trays of chicken a la king. We flew over more coffee fincas, more dense jungle, then past a volcano with lave-spattered sides.

Salvador, after nine hours in the air since Mexico City, at three in the afternoon. Army airplanes maneuvered over the field. Officials checked passports, vaccination certificates and our baggage. We passengers entered a car and started to town along a dusty, rutted road. Natives with wide straw hats walked along sucking stalks of sugar cane. Each carried a machete, a murderous looking knife with a curved, scythe-like blade. Some carried rifles as well as machetes. The driver told us the year before they found eighteen dead bodies at one spot beside the road and I was cheered to know that no revolution was in progress at the moment. Two-wheeled ox carts piled high with sugar cane lumbered down the center of the road and we gasped as our speed-mad driver swung around the narrow curves, each time missing a cart by inches.

San Salvador had rutted streets with white-washed adobe houses on either side. Pigs grunted in the dust as we tore past scattering dogs, chickens and children. We turned into a paved street holding a monument to a primitive Indian, feathered headdress and all. At the end of our hotel lobby a blue-tiled fountain dripped into a pool. On the closed dining room door was a sign "Comida 6:30". Three hours to wait and I was famished.

The plaster in our upstairs bedroom had nicks which my fertile imagination suspected were bullet holes. The room had no door, only a shutter affair across the opening to let in a maximum amount of air. High shuttered windows overlooked the plaza, across which was a 'teatro nationalle'. A cathedral wall was of corrugated iron, earthquake proof but unaesthetic. Ox carts creaked past. Black-shawled women hurried along and barefoot men carried straw baskets on their heads. A movie featuring Lionel Barrymore, with dialogue in Spanish, was advertised.

During the dinner hour a marimba band played. We had been up early, and must be up early again so we went right to bed, but not to sleep. A political banquet downstairs brought exuberant gentlemen congregating in the bar beneath, or talking on the sidewalk under our open windows. As I had just heard that no Salvadorian president had yet served a full term—either being assassinated or overthrown in a revolution—I was a bit uneasy about the banquet's outcome. We didn't sleep until after two and were called at the unearthly hour of three fifteen.

Early breakfast and a ride to the field in the dark, past lumbering ox carts, the car's horn blasting at every curve. Motors were warming up. The flight crew entered the terminal. Gongs sounded. We climbed aboard as the sky was tinged with color. I got a pillow and prepared to nap but the scenery was too engrossing. What a lot we miss nowadays when we fly at an altitude of 35,000 feet! Below were volcanoes with plumes of steam issuing from their craters. One small volcano, like an untidy child, had spewed black lava all down its sides. The pilot flew directly over one crater so we looked down into red hot slag.

A short stop in San Lorenzo, in Honduras. The pilot pointed out the direction of the road leading to Tegucigalpa. That's another 'someday' trip and another intriguing name. At least I've seen the way to Tegucigalpa! In Don Blanding's poem, "Names are Ships to Carry People" are the lines:

"Chests of carved and stained catalpa,

Letters from Tegucigalpa—"

Over wide blue Lake Managua, over the city of Managua with our Nicarauguan doctor telling stories of battles here before the days of U.S. Marine occupation. On the airport a small platoon of soldiers drilled at the edge of the field. We found a U.S. plane with a pilot acquaintance here on vacation. Everyone shook hands with us, and shook hands again when we left. Was this a Spanish custom or were the people unusually friendly?

After twenty minutes we were off again over jungles and farms, over more cultivated ground than heretofore seen in Central

America. Huge churches dominated all the small villages. At San Jose field in Costa Rica our bride-to-be was met by a plump fiance, a prospective mother-in-law, armloads of flowers, and cameras.

We ate again while flying over jungles, with the Pacific Ocean on our right. Another brief stop at David (pronounced Dah-veed), at a breathlessly hot station. My memory here is of the pilot drawing me outside to show me orchids growing in the trees.

More jungle, and then across the hills was Gatun Lake and ahead was the Panama Canal. We descended from 8000 feet to the city of Panama, down over big steamers, over red-roofed Army buildings and black-roofed hangars of the Army field, to land just above the tide flats. My camera was sealed so I couldn't take pictures of the canal which enemies might want. I'm sure there are detailed drawings of it in existence and that my snapshots wouldn't have helped anyone.

I wish that every school child in America might have a chance to take this twenty-minute flight across the Panama Canal from ocean to ocean. The Pacific behind us, the Atlantic ahead. Out over the city of Cristobal-Colon (named for Christopher Columbus)—Cristobal on the Panama republic side of the street, Colon on the American occupation side. A plane from South America was just landing.

We drove to town in an open car, on the left side of the road. In Jamaica we again encountered the left-hand drive, but that was British country where we expected it. I nearly had heart failure on every curve when cars whizzed by on the right. Since that I've lived with left-hand drive in New Zealand and Pakistan and, by constantly reminding myself to stay on the left, I've lived!

Four days were spent at the Canal Zone in the airy Hotel Washington by the edge of the Atlantic. We found more shuttered doors. Electric lights burned constantly in the closets to keep clothes from mildewing in the humidity. The heat was enervating, even though it was only March. Our clothes stuck to us; we took several showers a day and constantly mopped our brows. The air was muggy and oppressing.

We tripped to the Gatun Locks and went aboard a big liner docked there. I admired the swimming pools and luxurious fittings, but knew I preferred to travel on our one-class Alaskan ships with their friendly atmosphere.

While Joe worked I browsed in the Hindu-owned shops along Front Street, admiring beautiful linens from Manila and the Orient, exquisite silks, perfumes, Oriental treasures. There were no fixed prices and a customer was expected to bargain. This was my first experience in haggling. Years later in Hong Kong, a shop girl began lowering prices before I even had a chance to start dickering.

"One dollar, ma'am. Eighty cents, ma'am. How much you give, ma'am?"

I found an exquisite embroidered tablecloth with dinner size napkins and in three days succeeded in reducing the price from $30 to $18. I still felt I could not afford it. The day we were leaving Lon Cope flew in from Brownsville and we made a tour of the shops while Joe talked aviation with the rest of the crew. Lon selected some things for Margaret and I showed him the cloth I wanted. His purchases totalled $31 and he said, "Throw in that tablecloth and I'll give you forty dollars for the lot."

The clerk nearly wept, but we got the set and so I paid only $9 for my beautiful tablecloth—which I still cherish.

We visited cabarets where shopworn girls danced. The principal occupants were sailors on shore leave, interested in drinking and dancing girls. The Canal cities were once known as the wickedest cities in the world, with the possible exception of Singapore. A walk down through the huge red light district gave me a sick, unclean feeling. Everywhere were drunken sailors, some of them so young! "Join the Navy and see the World!"

So went our four days, shopping, sightseeing, dancing at the Stranger's Club.

Monday morning, March 6th, 1933. President Roosevelt had just been inaugurated. News came that U.S. banks had been closed. We could not cash a check. We had spent almost all of our money buying linens and a camera. How fortunate that we had passes on the airplane! We counted our money and figured that we had just enough to get to Miami, so we decided we better start north. It would be most embarrassing to be caught without any money in a foreign country.

Before daylight we were at the airport for the first leg of our return journey. Our baggage was weighed in and our purchases had increased its poundage. Weight is of prime consideration on airlines, especially on the big flying boats where much gasoline must be carried for long water flights. I had found it most difficult to plan clothes for this trip which began in a snowstorn near the Canadian border and was now in the heat of the tropics.

The Commodore accommodated twenty-four people, the largest airplane I had ever been in. It was pushed into the water by a crew of men in bathing trunks. The beaching gear was detached, and we took off across the waves over the most northern tip of South America.

Head winds slowed us and the flight was rough. We were an hour behind schedule. Fog hid the sight of land except for an infrequent rocky headland or a patch of tangled jungle. I stretched out on a bunk and tried to fight off airsickness. If Dramamine had been invented I hadn't found it yet.

Our schedule called for an hour's layover at Baranquilla, Colombia but we were late and the Clipper which was to take us north across the Caribbean was warming up when we landed. My impressions of South America are meager as we stopped only ten minutes. I walked through the terminal and stepped outside so I may say I have set foot on South American soil. I remember a wide, muddy river, a low-roofed town, a group of airplanes painted in zig-zag stripes for camouflage (a war was then going on with a neighboring country over some border rights). Officials at the terminal conversed in German, part of Barranquilla's large German population. Lunch was ordered for us but we had no time to eat it.

The Clipper was then the biggest passenger plane in service in America. It carried 37 passengers and a flight crew of seven. It seemed more like a flying Pullman coach, or a yacht, than an airplane. The compartments had upholstered seats for eight. The paneled walls were hung with attractive wood cuts, depicting the progress of transportation form ox cart to airplane. There were curtains at the windows, ladies' and men's lavatories, a smoking room—the last word in air comfort. What a contrast to the old Jennie with its open cockpit and cruising range of about two hours! Compartment doors were bulkheaded so that in case of a forced landing in the sea they could be closed and the compartment would be water tight. As I looked out of the window at the massive wing, as I heard the drone of the four giant motors, I felt such security that it seemed impossible any emergency would arise. The plane rode through the air smoothly, evenly.

Our flight was six hours across the Caribbean to Jamaica. The steward brought a card table to set between us so we could write letters or play cribbage 5000 feet above the ocean. But Joe couldn't sit still and kept poking his nose up into the pilot's compartment, wanting to see the workings of the big flying boat, wanting to study the instrument panel.

The Caribbean was the testing ground for Pan American Airways pilots, the college where they earned their advanced degrees. Here they put into practice the principles of navigation and meteorology which they would use later on ocean flights across the Pacific and the Atlantic—routes which were still only in the planning stage. Three years later Joe would himself be captaining one of these huge planes on this run, training for his transfer to the Pacific.

At six o'clock we circled the harbor at Kingston, Jamaica, and landed beside a float anchored in the water. Through customs and immigrations where officials seemed to be searching for American cigarettes. A launch took passengers and crew ashore and a waiting taxi hurried us into town—on the left side of the streets.

The Myrtle Bank Hotel did not want to accept our American money and charged us $15 for our dinner and a very ordinary room for the night. Our dwindling dollars were discounted. A month later the hotel sent us a check to make up the difference between their regular charge and what we had been charged—after the rate of exchange was settled and our banks opened. But that didn't help us then.

The hotel was attractively situated, with green lawns and walks leading to the water's edge. The dining room was very formal; we saw more dinner jackets than we had seen in all other stops together. This city was British, and British anywhere in the world dress for dinner, we'd heard. Prices were in pounds and shillings. After dinner we walked in the soft, warm night, delighting in the British accents of the black people. But it had been a long, long day so we retired early and saw little of Kingston.

A morning flight took us across the island, above plantation homes and green fields, then over small islands almost awash in the waves. Up the west coast of Cuba to land at noon at Cienfuegos. Strong winds made docking difficult, but eventually we went ashore and ate our lunches in the terminal where places were set, ready for us. At each place was a red rose, and a bottle of local beer instead of coffee.

Two hours more across Cuba, over neat plantations where ox-teams worked in the fields, guided by men in loose cotton garments and huge straw hats.

We soared over historic Morro Castle, over the city of Havana, and came down in the harbor just as a torrential rain storm burst and blotted out visibility. At last we dashed ashore in the midst of it, had our baggage inspected, and rode up town in a comfortable Pan-Am bus. As we left the terminal the rain stopped and the Clipper took off for Miami, less than two hours away. (Of course this was long before the days of Fidel Castro!)

A sightseeing tour took us around Havana, which I remember as a clean, pleasant city. We toured past historic buildings, attractive residential areas, cigar factories, a convent with a high wall in which was a window where we were told unwanted babies could be deposited. The taxi driver suggested a night club tour for the evening but a $3 tourist charge had reduced our money so alarmingly we could not afford any extra entertainment. Instead we ate dinner quietly at the hotel and watched rhumba dancers perform a rhumba with the tuba playing 'down in Cuba'.

Next afternoon we crossed blue sunlit waters to Miami, in a plane loaded to capacity, over small keys appearing just above the surface of the waves. Fifteen minutes after we landed our baggage was inspected, our customs declaration filed, and we were free to go into the city. Miami's Pan American terminal demonstrated streamlined efficiency in performing official red tape necessary at a port of entry.

A friend of Joe's met us and drove us along palm-bordered streets which were bright with scarlet hibiscus blooms, oleanders, and other tropical flowers. We saw lovely homes which in summer were boarded up by their wealthy owners as they followed the seasons to other resorts.

Less than a dollar in cash remained of our money—much too little for comfort—when we registered at a hotel on Biscayne Boulevard, but here we could get credit and could sign for our meals since Joe was an employee of Pan American Airways.

After a few days the banks opened and we could get money again.

CHAPTER THIRTEEN

Still Up in the Air

Two weeks we were in Miami, lazy days for me while Joe studied at the terminal buildings. In the evenings we walked along the waterfront admiring the yachts and pretending to choose one. We drove a rented car to Coral Gables to watch an autogyro (today we call them helicopters) land on the Miami-Biltmore Hotel Golf Course. At sunset one evening we watched the Akron moor as it returned from a trip to Panama.

At an airport where palmetto grew from the sand and coral rock I flew an hour or two in a little Aeronca. Joe hated watching me, protesting that the tiny plane wasn't safe to fly, and that anyway it wasn't safe with me flying it.

The Pan American Airways staff was very friendly. We went to a show with Captain and Mrs. Ed Musick; Ed Musick was then chief pilot. Mrs. Musick invited me to a luncheon where I met several company wives. We lunched with the operations manager, and had a fishing trip out into the Gulf Stream with Mr. and Mrs. Dutton. Mr. Dutton was the division manager. Never a good sailor, I was desperately seasick and didn't care whether I lived or died.

March 25th we boarded a Clyde Mallory liner, the "Algonquin", bound for New York. While still at the dock we had a pleasant dinner at the captain's table. That was my last meal until we reached New York. I'm sure it was the roughest trip in the history of the ocean and that the ship tried gymnastics. If I have to cross oceans I want to be in a jet plane doing six hundred miles an hour.

I did get up three days later to watch the ship enter the harbor, past the Statue of Liberty. The weather was cold and rainy, with gusts of snow. New York looked even dirtier than I remembered it, and my head ached from the incessant noise of street traffic, subways, elevators and people.

We saw some good shows, and I purchased my first formal, of black chiffon. I also bought a velvet evening wrap, long black gloves, and an evening bag, and Joe bought me my first corsage, one of gardenias. Feeling like Mrs. Astor's plush horse, I went with him to dinner at the home of an aviation great and later to see Ed Wynn and to hear his Fire Chief broadcast.

Joe had work to do, and I had children across the continent. New

120

York wasn't my kind of life, so within a week I took a train, westbound. Snow still lay on the frozen fields, on Iowan corn stalks and the Nebraska prairies.

At Sterling, Colorado, I left the train and spent five wonderful days with old friends I hadn't seen for fifteen years. But Colorado was in its dust bowl years. Trees our homesteading fathers had planted had dried up and blown away. Dust blew incessantly; tumbleweeds rolled across the prairie and piled up along the barbed wire fences. Dust sifted through windows and settled on dishes, beds and tables.

The one-room schoolhouse where I began school was replaced by a modern consolidated school and a gymnasium replaced the stable where we tied up our horses. School buses replaced horses. I talked to the children at the school, sons and daughters of old schoolmates of mine, telling them that when I went to school there I had certainly never dreamed of flying to Alaska or to South America—so they couldn't tell what might be in store for them either.

Snow was falling as friends took me back to Sterling across the sand hills. On the South Platte River bridge I recalled how Dad used to drive in from the farm with his team of white horses, and how frightened I used to be to come to town. This time Sterling didn't seem so overwhelming—not after New York's crowds.

Over treeless plains, over the Rockies, along the Snake River where the Old Oregon Trail ran. Easter morning I woke in the Columbia River gorge and saw green trees, ferns, wild currant and trilliums in bloom.

"Isn't this lovely?" I exclaimed to the porter.

"Yes, ma'am," he agreed enthusiastically. "Dis heah suah am God's country!"

The children looked well, healthy and rosy-cheeked, and daffodils and tulips were in bloom between Bellingham and Lynden.

We again rented the three-room apartment on Lynden's Main Street. Teddy went on the bus to Bellingham with me where I took ten hours of flight time in an OX5 Waco at the old Graham airport, in order to renew my private license. A new Department of Commerce ruling then required private pilots to have fifty hours of solo and as I had only twenty-five I let my license go. Flying was too expensive for a hobby. But in learning to fly I had proved for my own satisfaction that I could do it and that there weren't really any outstanding sexual differences in the abilities.

Weeks dragged on and Joe was no nearer to a permanent assignment. School ended and Margie Lou was promoted to the third grade. We went to Portland to visit my sister and I rented another apartment there, so when fall came I could put both children in school, Teddy as a first grader.

Our Model A Ford had been stored all this time in Fairbanks so we finally sold it and I bought a new car in Seattle, asking to have the license sent to Portland.

Mother and Dad Barrows came to visit us and I drove them up the Columbia River Highway. We parked at Multnomah Falls to climb up to the bridge. When I came back to the car a highway patrolman was standing beside it. He pointed to the "Washington license applied for" sticker on the windshield and asked, "You live in Portland?"

"Yes."

"Then why are you buying a Washington license for your car?"

"Well," I started to explain. "I don't realy live in Portland. I'm just visiting my sister there."

"Then where do you live?"

"I live in Alaska."

"Still," he persisted, "how come you are getting a Washington license?"

Again I attempted an explanation. "You see, I came out of Alaska, bought my car in Seattle, and now I'm visiting in Portland until I go back north."

"Hm-m-m," he was dubious. "Let's see your driver's license."

Alaska didn't require them so all I had was a California one!

Mother and Dad had been listening with interest. "Why didn't you just tell him you live on the Pacific Coast and let it go at that?" Dad asked.

Someway the Richfield Reporter got hold of the story and told it, with embellishments, over the radio—a woman with an Oregon address, a Washington license on her car, a California driver's license, who said she actually lived in Alaska. I was ribbed about my police record and, thinking another officer might not be so friendly, I bought an Oregon car license and got a new Oregon driver's license. I had my first one at age 16, in Ashland, when all you had to do was send 25¢ in to the State Department which issued them—no driving test.

It was October before Joe flew through on his way to deliver two Fleetsters to Alaska. He had flown directly from Miami, accompanied by Joe Crosson—another Alaskan pilot. They stayed over a day in Portland because of weather so Joe did have a brief visit with his children. It had been ten months since they had seen each other, and over six months since I had seen my husband.

On his return he took a two week's vacation to spend with us. We went to the beach, played golf, and spent every minute they weren't in school with the children. Then Joe went back to Miami.

We had Christmas in Portland, this time with my family instead of being alone somewhere. In January, 1934, Joe flew north again. These flights from Miami to Fairbanks weren't easy ones, although his health was much better. He left the sub-tropics, went through snowstorms in Utah and Nevada, rain on the coast, and in five or six days was in sub-zero of Arctic winter. It was 40 degrees below in Fairbanks.

My cousin and her husband were managing the apartment house where we stayed. Depression victims from the mid-West, they had recently moved to Oregon. Neither of us had much money so we used to attend any free lectures which sounded interesting.

One evening we went to hear a 'numerologist', who called himself a 'soul unfolder'. He selected members of the audience and asked names and birth dates. These he wrote on a blackboard, added and subtracted, and told them what they might expect of life—briefly, as his regular reading cost two dollars. He pointed to me and when I told him my first name he said, "I'm sorry for you. I'm sorry for all women named Mary. The Marys bear the burdens of the world. They are the big sisters, the ones who help bring up the others and loan them money."

I knew at once he must be pretty good as I was the oldest of seven children.

"This has been a negative year for you," he went on. "But 1936 will see you settled. You've been very unsettled so far," (That wasn't any news to me!) "I see you living down on the lower east coast somewhere."

I decided he wasn't so good after all. I didn't want to live on the lower east coast, which I figured could mean Miami.

In February Joe wired from Fairbanks that he was renting a six-room house with garage, greenhouse and good water. We were to come north. He was to be assigned back in Fairbanks. It seemed too good to be true; to be settled again after fourteen months of separation, of living in furnished apartments. How wonderful to have a home again, with our own things around us.

Quickly I washed clothes, ironed and packed. Then I made a hurried drive to Southern California to see Dad and Mother Barrows and Grandpa Noyes. My brother, Frank, was living in Carmel and we spent two days in that delightful town.

Wires from Joe followed me, first telling me to come on north, and then telling me to stay where I was.

President Roosevelt had cancelled all airmail contracts and aviators were unsure of their futures. Six army pilots were killed in those few days, carrying mail on unfamiliar routes, in unfamiliar planes, on night flights for which they were not trained while the men who knew these jobs were forced to sit idly on the ground.

Still waiting for a wire from Joe, we drove up to Lynden and I almost shed tears of envy as I saw Dick and Marion's new house. It seemed hopeless ever to plan for a home of my own.

At last a wire arrived telling us to catch the ship which sailed Saturday morning from Seattle. Golf clubs which Joe had given me would not fit in my trunk. There was the beginning of a golf course in Anchorage; there might be one in Fairbanks so I decided to carry the clubs.

My youngest sister, Dorothy, was going north with me this time as the home situation with our stepmother was not a happy one. We sailed on the old "Victoria" and it wasn't a pleasure liner; neither was March a month when tourists took excursions to Alaska. Dottie had a room with an old lady somewhere aft and the children and I were assigned a stateroom with triple bunks, Teddy in the top. Our stateroom opened onto the deck. The social hall was down inside and there was no observation room.

We encountered rough water before we left Seattle harbor and our whole trip was unpleasant. It was only 20 degrees above zero at Wrangell. The tide was wrong and we had to wait to go through the Narrows. A blizzard was blowing at Juneau where we docked to unload lumber and we were tied up there all day. The Vic went on up to Skagway and returned to dock again at Juneau for some reason. We were nine days to Seward, thirty-six hours in the Gulf of Alaska and the children and I were seasick every minute of that thirty-six hours. A fog bank at Yakutat forced us to lie outside in the Gulf nine hours before we could go in. Dottie vowed she'd stay in Alaska the rest of her life if the only way out was by ship.

Finally we docked at Seward in midafternoon and made connections with the train for Anchorage. Joe met us there and took us to a hotel.

Our delight in seeing him quickly faded when we found he was on his way 'outside', catching the same ship we had just left, and heading for New York. It didn't seem right, or fair. I wept most of the night and at the moment hated big companies.

But this time we were coming home, home to a roomy two-story house at the end of Cushman Street. Our furniture had been brought out of storage and the dining room and living room were piled with trunks and crates which had been stored for over two years. What fun to open the boxes and see things I'd almost forgotten that we owned.

The children went to school, greeting old friends of their kindergarten days. Teddy's teacher in the first grade was Miss Anne Hopkins, who later married one of the Flying Wien brothers. Dottie enrolled in the Fairbanks High School, upstairs in the grade school building.

Fairbanks, in those days before the war and before rapid transportation (and before the pipe-line), was one of the friendliest towns in the world.

"Glad to see you back in Fairbanks again," the milkman greeted me.

A neighbor brought a bowl of stew and some hot rolls.

The children enjoyed their freedom after living in a Portland apartment. Now they played in the street on their new sled, getting out of the way for an occasional dog team or wood truck to go by. The water wagon had a stovepipe which puffed smoke, the stove burning to keep the bottled water from freezing. Sometimes a horse-drawn sled passed, the horses wearing strings of sleigh bells. Most cars were in cold storage for the winter. Ours was still in Seattle.

At the airport I saw the gang of Nenana days, working now in a modern new hangar with well equipped shop—a far cry from the wallboard structure down on the Tanana River ice.

We went to Sunday School and church. I joined the P.T.A., renewed acquaintances and made new friends. I loved stopping to visit with neighbors as I walked uptown, as I'm essentially a small-town person. This time we were going to put down those roots we had always longed to plant. It was time they got into the soil before they withered and died.

As spring came the snow melted and turned to slush. Teddy fell into the mud several times a day and needed clean corduroys. I bought red rubber boots and both children tried to be amphibians. The ice went out at 2:07 on the 30th of April.

Two Russian aviators, Levenoffsky and Slepnov, arrived to purchase two of the Fleetsters Joe ferried north. These were flown to Nome where the Russians aided in rescuing a group of their countrymen who were stranded on an ice floe in Bering Sea. Levenoffsky later came over Fairbanks in a record-making flight across the North Pole. In 1937 he was lost somewhere in the Arctic wastes.

I planted radishes and lettuce in my greenhouse. We had fresh rhubarb from our own plants. Sunday afternoon we hiked out the trail toward the Tanana River, out the Richardson Highway, anywhere just to be outside in the spring air, though after the break-up the mosquitoes were out and tried to eat us alive.

One mid-summer's day Margie Lou and Teddy decided to stay up all night to see the midnight sun. I agreed. It was light all night, bright daylight. Around one o'clock I told them to stay in the yard and play quietly as neighbors were asleep and I was going to bed.

"You're going to bed and leave us up?" they were surprised that I'd desert them.

Soon afterward they decided they might as well go to bed, not because they were tired, but there wasn't anyone to play with. But of course they weren't tired!

I took some flying time in a Monocoupe but it cracked up near Mt. McKinley.

"Why are you taking flying lessons?" asked Teddy. "You could crack up without any lessons, couldn't you?"

Flying was just too expensive as a hobby, and it couldn't be anything else at that time.

July 1st the thermometer registered 102°. In the greenhouse I had tomato vines covered with tomatoes, cucumber vines heavy with potential pickles and three pepper plants, all thriving. We had radishes and lettuce. The children played under the sprinkler in bathing suits. We might have been in Southern California.

Joe left New York on June 27th, flying north in a Ford freighter by way of interior Canada—north over Winnepeg, Lake Athabasca, Great Bear Lake, Great Slave Lake, down the Mackenzie River to Aklavik on the Arctic, and then across into Alaska. Canadian regulations prohibited the use of his radio, so we could not hear from him.

July 3rd we drove out to Harding Lake, fifty miles east of Fairbanks, where he would land the big freighter. Rain had washed away the dust. White-trunked birches lined the road, purple fireweed and pink wild roses bloomed everywhere. Harding Lake was blue as we drove down to the water's edge where the huge airplane, with gleaming aluminum finish, had lighted.

Al Monsen, who had flown from New York with Joe, was standing on a pontoon. He wore a straw hat which he took off for me to admire.

"I bought this in little old New York," he said.

Looking around at the hills he added, "Gee-zus, I never expected to get here. I couldn't work on the maps with Joe, it looked so far from New York to Fairbanks. You can have your subways and your Coney Islands—give me the good old Kuskokwim River valley every time."

The route they had flown would conjure up mental pictures for Joe of a heavy plane which would not take off well from smooth water, of friendly Mounted Policemen, of the cooperation of the airmen of the Northern Canada Airlines, and of faraway places and thousands of miles of uninhabited country stretching around the northern part of the continent. This had been another pioneering exploration flight, as Lindbergh's had been, along the Great Circle Course.

The children were wildly happy to see their daddy, and to know that after more than two years of constant separation, he was home

126

to stay.
    At least for awhile!

CHAPTER FOURTEEN

Wife of a Bush Pilot

Our car was shipped from Seattle to Valdez. We caught a ride over the Richardson Highway with a company truck. Valdez did not suffer from the exorbitant freight rates the Alaska Railroad charged on merchandise to Fairbanks, so we bought cases of groceries and piled them in the truck. Before starting back we had fresh peaches with real cream—not from a can of milk with two holes punched in the top, which invariably sat on a restaurant counter.

It was good to have a car again and we drove slowly, enjoying the scenery. At Summit Lake Joe stopped to go fishing. As we started again an ancient Buick careened around the corner on the wrong side of a hairpin turn and crashed into our radiator. Our only casualties were black and blue bruises, but our car's fender and radiator shell were smashed flat. The Buick's windshield was splintered and a passenger was badly cut. We bandaged him as best we could and started to town with him, his fishing trip ended abruptly. The steering gear was damaged and the front wheels out of line so we proceeded very carefully. At three in the morning we delivered our patient to the hospital.

I got out our insurance policy and found, in fine print, that it was not good in Alaska. The repair bills were $175.

Two young writers from the east, Corey Ford and Alistair MacBain, were fishing at Stuart Lake in British Columbia. Joe was instructed to pick them up and bring them to Fairbanks. They were gathering material for an article on fishing. I got Ford's "Salt Water Taffy" from the library, and also read his article on sea serpents—so I could converse intelligently with these authors.

Joe said I might accompany them on a flight to Nome and I was overjoyed to get down the Yukon again. We flew low over ponds where moose, bear and caribou were feeding and landed at Manley Hot Springs for the night. Our eastern writers were surprised at the profusion and size of flowers growing there.

At Tanana we inspected the old fort buildings. We lunched at Ruby and stopped for the night at Nulato. Father MacElmeel hurried down to greet us warmly.

"One of the Indian boys told me you were here," he said. "He ran up saying 'Joe is here'. 'Joe Crosson?' I asked. 'No, no, the

Joe with red hair!"

We stayed at the mission with our good host and his assistant, young Father O'Connor, formerly an athletic coach and proud of his Nulato baseball team. In the morning I visited the sweet-faced sisters and toured the new schoolhouse.

Across the tundra to Nome, past cliffs where countless birds wheeled and circled. White beluga whales dived in the blue waters below us.

The King Island Eskimoes were in and we met Father LaFortune who lived on the island with them. They came eighty miles across Bering Sea in frail skin umiaks. We watched them making ivory paper knives, cribbage boards and curios to trade to local merchants for their winter supplies.

The "Victoria" anchored in the open roadstead while we were there, bringing Nome's first tourists since the beginning of the depression. The Eskimoes performed for the benefit of the tourists, tossing up members of their group, or willing bystanders, in a walrus skin blanket. Kayak races were run through the low-rolling breakers. In the evening we were again fortunate in seeing the Wolf Dance, a performance similar to the one which had honored the Lindberghs.

Three weeks later Nome burned to the ground. Gone were the buildings dating back to the gold rush. Gone was the Golden Gate Hotel once resplendent with fancy furniture but which I remembered for uneven floors and lumpy mattresses. The old saloons with swinging doors were burned, the wooden sidewalks warped by successive frosts and thaws, the banker's modern apartment which once boasted the only flush toilet in Nome. The fire made a clean sweep from the beach back to the tundra.

Joe was home most of the time that summer, making only short trips.

School started in September and Dottie was elected president of the junior class. I attended PTA, went to bridge parties, assisted at a Ladies Aid bazaar and taught a Sunday School class. We began to feel that we were really part of Fairbanks, that this was our home town.

Joe decided we might begin planning to build a house. We selected lots near the airport where the water was good—for Fairbanks. I drew plans for a small log house, which would be easy to heat, with bedrooms up under the eaves for the children. Would my dreams finally materialize? After ten years of married life, would I at last have a home?

We picked berries and made jam and jelly. We went caribou hunting along the Steese Highway. Our caribou and a moose quarter were cut into roasts and steaks and frozen. Often we dined on spruce hens, ptarmigan and ducks, living from the fat of the land.

But this family interlude was too good to last. In October Joe was called south to bring up a Lockheed Electra, expecting to be gone about a month.

Immediately after he left I discovered that I was pregnant. After Teddy's birth the doctor had said I shouldn't have another Caesarean section.

"Isn't it better to live to bring up the two you have," he said, "than to kill yourself trying to have a third child?"

I was nauseated every morning—I, who had not missed a day of school before Margie Lou's birth. I dragged down to the basement to build the furnace fire and as the days grew colder I stoked the furnace, emptied the ashes, got meals for my family. At night I often lay awake, afraid of dying and leaving my children motherless. And Joe was gone nearly three months.

Our spindly Christmas tree shed its needles as it thawed. Our turkey stayed frozen in the 'cache' and we spent a lonely Christmas, the children's sixth in succession without their father. The water pump froze in the basement and I kept a kettle full of hot water on the kitchen range to use in thawing it. Christmas Day it was 30° below zero.

Before New Year's Day Joe landed in a beautiful twin-motored Electra, the biggest transport plane the Alaskan interior had yet seen.

January was bitterly cold and our house was cold. We burned a ton of coal a week and I knew how much that was as I shoveled it into the furnace and shoveled out the ashes. The pump froze daily. At that time Fairbanks had no central water system and each house had its own well.

A flu epidemic struck the town and schools, public meetings, and the theater were closed. All of us were ill. There were four hundred cases in town and it was ten o'clock one night before the weary doctor got to us. He told Joe that I had better go 'outside'.

I had written to my cousins in Lynden telling them we had the flu. When Dick got the letter he immediately sent a telegram telling me to come to them. The wire reached us on Tuesday and Saturday morning we were aboard a plane bound for Skagway. It was 30° below when we took off from Fairbanks that February morning. We made an overnight stop in Whitehorse, staying at the Whitehorse Inn. Then we followed the historic trail of '98 over the White Pass and Yukon Railroad, circling over Everett Wasson's plane, resting on the ice at Carcross. In fancy I could see the toiling throngs of gold seekers who had climbed over that plass on their way in to the Klondike.

The temperature at Skagway was 32° above, just freezing. At the Pullen Hotel pans of milk adorned the table and nothing ever tasted better.

The little 'Princess Norah', on which I had made my first trip north, seemed palatial to us. The food was delicious and the fresh milk, salads and fruits all did me a world of good. I wasn't sick another minute. Crocuses were blooming and the grass was green at Alert Bay and when we reached Lynden we saw daffodils and tulips, the air was warm, and I decided that I might live after all.

Dick had rented the same three-room apartment which we had lived in before. Margie Lou was in school with old friends. Every day I walked at least a mile, ate fresh vegetables and drank newly churned buttermilk. Dr. Marion LeCocq took charge of me, an arrangement combining friendship and the ability of a competent surgeon.

Two weeks after we arrived we received letters from Fairbanks. Mine from Joe and Dottie told about the Ice Carnival. Margie's, from girl friends, began: "My, wasn't it too bad your house burned down. It was a terrible fire. We went out the next day to see what was left, and it surely looked awful."

At once I wired asking for details. My answer read as follows: "How the hell did you find out stop neighbors saved some of our personal effects and my accordion stop writing details love."

Alaska had no airmail then so it was two weeks before we knew whether we owned a thing in the world besides Joe's accordion. He and Dottie had decided not to worry me and so hadn't written about the fire.

The fire apparently started when a smoldering coal popped out of the furnace. It burned up through the dining room and living room floors, ruining our rugs, the grand piano, radio, half my books, almost everything in the two rooms. Upstairs our linens and clothing were scorched and stained with chemical. When the fire was out water froze on the furniture and the finish peeled and checked. Never was such a soggy, charred, smelly mess. Neighbors dried clothing in their own homes. Then everything was stacked in the garage to await our return.

The landlord had insurance to repair the house. We had none. Now there was no home waiting for me when I came back, if I came back. Of course, my expensive trip, my coming operation and the fire shelved any plans to build a house.

June 12th, on Margie's ninth birthday, I went into surgery. Joe flew out and Mother Barrows came from Los Angeles to stay with the children. It took a long time to fight back to daylight, to the conscious world. But I was alive, and I had a beautiful little daughter, Mary Jo.

Teddy had stoutly maintained great indifference. He didn't want a little sister; he would rather have a puppy. And what good were girls, anyway? But when the nurse led them to the glass-walled nursery and held up their new baby sister Ted lost his heart. The little round head and big brown eyes won him immediately and when the nurse exclaimed, "Why, the baby looks just like you!" his subjugation was complete.

Six weeks later we sailed north. The baby was a perfect traveler and most tourists never knew there was such a young passenger aboard. We landed at Valdez, where our new car was unloaded, and drove to Fairbanks over the Richardson Highway. It was midnight when we reached town and we had difficulty in restraining Teddy from shouting the good news that he had returned.

The new house Joe had rented at Eleventh and Lacey, wasn't quite finished but the old one was sold and we were asked to clear the garage. Dottie and I worked for days sorting the mess of charred clothing, dishes coated with chemical stains, pieces of furniture with peeling finish, water-stained rugs with holes in the middle. Anything we might salvage was taken over to the new house. We bought some new pieces of furniture and moved in.

During this time everyone else in town was driving out to the Chena Slough to watch a low-wing plane land and to stand entranced as an aviator with a patch over one eye and a genial man in gray trousers and old brown coat climbed out. Teddy and his pals were right in front and managed to stand beside Wiley Post as hundreds of cameras took pictures of him and Will Rogers.

As the noted actor and humorist walked around town he might, because of his unassuming manner and his informal clothes, have been a miner in from the creeks. Children clustered around and Mr. Rogers signed autographs for all of them. I drove Joe out to the field one morning and there met our distinguished travelers. Rogers' humor was easy and spontaneous. He noted Joe Crosson's new Chrysler and our new Ford.

"Sure is prosperous up here with the Democrats," he said. "See those new cars."

Just then an old jaloppie rattled up, scarcely able to hold together.

"How do you account for that one?" I asked.

"Oh, that's left over from the Republicans," he answered quickly.

Alaska's two "flying Joes" took the illustrious visitors on a flight to the Matanuska Valley and on to Anchorage. Will Rogers' daily column commented:

WILL ROGERS SAYS:

132

Anchorage, Alaska, Aug. 15—To the Editor of the Herald: Well we had a day off yesterday and nothing to do so we went flying with friends, Joe Crosson, Alaska's crack pilot, who is a great friend of Wiley's and helped him on his difficulties up here on his record flights, and Joe Barrows, another fine pilot, in a Lockheed Electra.

We scaled Mount McKinley, the highest one of the North American continent. Bright, sunny day and the most beautiful sight I ever saw. Crosson has landed on a glacier half way up in a plane and took off. Flew right over hundreds of mountain sheep. Flew low over moose and bear down in the valley. Now to visit the Matanuska Valley, where they sent 1935 model pioneers.

Yours,
WILL ROGERS

This was almost the last "Will Rogers Says."

When I went to the field in the evening I carried the baby with me. Rogers was standing in the administration office talking about Matanuska.

"Sure is a great country for babies," he observed. "There are fifty or so already in the Matanuska Valley and that many more on the way. Why," turning to look at Mary Jo, "here's one that wasn't here this morning!"

Dottie and I moved into the new house. Mechanics brought the company truck and helped carry the furniture, some of which had been refinished by a cabinet maker.

That day Post and Rogers went out to Harding Lake where mechanics gassed and oiled their plane for a flight to Point Barrow and watched them head into the north. A weather report from Barrow told of ground fog there but Joe could not communicate with the lake to give Wiley Post the report before he took off.

Next morning Joe left for Juneau to pick up passengers for a flight to Dawson for a Discovery Day celebration. A few minutes later Teddy ran into the house.

"Mother!" he shouted, "Jerry Nerland just told me he heard that Will Rogers and Wiley Post crashed near Point Barrow."

Fairbanks was stunned. Joe Crosson brought the bodies down from the Arctic slopes. Telegrams poured in from everywhere. People realized how well loved Will Rogers had been.

On top of this tragedy Fairbanks experienced another. Art Hines, a private pilot, was missing with three passengers on the way back from Dawson. Seventeen planes searched without avail. During the search Hines's partner, Percy Hubbard, crashed and his plane was burned. Almost a year later the twisted and burned fuselage of the Hines plane was discovered accidentally by a miner.

A regular Sunday service to Juneau was inaugurated, and on Sunday mornings we took Joe to the airport. The big silver Electra was wheeled out and crowds watched the beginning of the weekly flight. Onlookers might be a bishop of the Episcopal church, business men in fur coats, prospectors in mukluks and mackinaws, Indians, children loitering on their way to Sunday School, all watching this miracle of modern transportation.

Five hours from Fairbanks to Juneau, instead of five to seven days. No wonder old timers watched respectfully as the motors were turned up, as Joe came out dressed in his new blue uniform, with his cap jauntily worn on his red hair, accompanied by a uniformed co-pilot. A starting flag fluttered down. The motors roared and the plane swung into the air, headed toward the Canadian Yukon.

Then I drove home to get breakfast, send Margie Lou and Teddy to Sunday School, bathe the baby and fix her formula of canned milk and corn syrup. Monday night, when Joe stayed over in Juneau, was my bridge-playing night with a group of young mothers. And so busy, happy days slipped by. Busy because I did the housework in a seven-room house (with help from Dottie and Margie Lou after school hours), washed clothes and cooked for six persons. I even baked my own bread. But I was happy because we were settled. The baby was healthy and happy and all the family loved her.

"I just couldn't get tired of her, or think she could grow up to be a nuisance," Margie declared passionately. But big sisters sing a different tune when babies begin to toddle about and get into things.

At Christmas Joe was with us for the first time in years. On Christmas Eve we went to the Catholic church for the midnight mass service. Outside in the still cold night, with moonlight making the snow shine, we thought of Christmas in warmer lands—everywhere, everywhere, Christmas tonight.

In Los Angeles Mother Barrows read the weather reports and worried about a baby in a house when the weather was 30° below zero. Then it was forty, and fifty, and one morning it was 62° below. Smoke hung in a fog over town, the air crackled, frost built up on nailheads around key holes. Tree trunks drooped under their load of ice. When the doors were opened cold air vapored in along the floor; a temperature change of 130° existed between the indoors and the outdoors.

Winters are long in the interior of Alaska. The sun does not rise above the horizon for more than a month. Electric light bills mount. But in this house I had a servant, an automatic stoker for the furnace, an Iron Fireman, working day and night. How I enjoyed hearing it in the middle of the night while I nestled under the blankets. I didn't have to set the alarm for two a.m. to go down to shovel coal to keep the pipes from freezing before morning.

My chum, Violet, of high school and university days, who had ridden horseback with me all over southern Oregon, came to Fairbanks as a stenographer. I think we talked constantly for a week after she arrived, catching up on the intervening years since college.

The Fairbanks Ice Carnival in March was exciting with dog derbies, parades and the crowning of Miss Alaska on a throne of ice. Margie Lou danced in a recital in the Pioneer's Hall and sister Dottie played on the high school basketball team. We saw curling teams send heavy rocks sliding over the ice, and watched an ice hockey game.

One morning I received a telegram from the New York Times, asking me to go to the Matanuska Valley to write a story about the year-old colony, writing from the standpoint of an Alaskan.

I hired a woman to take care of the family, borrowed Joe's big camera, and caught the train. Slim Johnson from Nenana was now depot agent at Palmer and I wired him that I wanted to see as much of the colony as possible between trains.

When we emerged on the flat I couldn't believe that I was still in Alaska instead of Wisconsin or North Dakota. Here was a neat white farmhouse in the middle of a plowed field, then another and another. Chickens scratched in the yards, pigs rooted among the stubble, cows stood chewing their cuds.

I stood on the depot platform and gazed, amazed, first at the Chugach mountain range rimming the valley, then at the imposing array of new buildings—hospital, schoolhouse, community building, dormitories, the Trading Post. This was a real town, a planned town of orderly streets, so different from our haphazard mining towns.

Slim and Clara Johnson gave me a delicious lunch and then a man drove us around the colony along muddy roads—but roads. In 1936 few Alaskan roads really went anywhere. At comfortable log cabins we stopped to visit colonists, hearing praise from farmers who had been crushed by drought and depression and were now beginning to hope. They praised the mild winter of Alaska's 'banana belt', the rich soil, the possibilities of making a new life. At one house we had cake with real whipped cream, not canned cream. I wanted to move the whole Pan American Airways base to the Matanuska Valley.

Next day I was taken on another drive, then listened while a stenographer gave me statistics. I visited the hospital and talked with the doctor. Jack Allman, in his tent newspaper office, showed me mimeographed sheets of Palmer's newspaper. Everyone was helpful, anxious that the outside world get a true picture of Alaska in place of the polar bear and igloo publicity it usually received.

At last Don Erwin, head of the agricultural experimental station, drove me to Wasilla to catch the northbound train. I made hurried shorthand notes as he talked, and on the train I caught my breath and marveled at what I had seen. Activity—the air was full of the sound of axes, hammers, tractors, bulldozers. Ambition. Energy. Above all, hope. Here was something new, big, worthwhile, perhaps a preparation for Alaska's statehood. I could write my story with enthusiasm.

After frost was out of the ground we planted a garden, flowers, vegetables, and a whole patch of potatoes. Mary Jo took her first steps. Our radishes came up. Joe and I again got out the log cabin plans and talked seriously about starting to build a house.

Then, like a bomb bursting, came a wire from New York to this effect: "Lay off all but eight men as we are curtailing operations in the north. Joe Crosson will be manager. You are transferred to Miami, Florida, to fly there, your transfer to take effect immediately."

Just like that. Like a tree uprooted in a sudden windstorm. Why, Fairbanks was home! We had planted a garden, we were going to build a house.

Then this—

CHAPTER FIFTEEN

Mushing to Miami

Our furniture was sold, every piece. The car, our new piano, my recently acquired washing machine and mangle. Would I ever again have the heart to acquire possessions? All we took with us was a box of books, a barrel of dishes, two or three trunks and a bundle of bedding.

Violet decided to go with us to help me drive. An expert stenographer, she could obtain a position anywhere, possibly in South America. And sister Dottie, just graduated from Fairbanks High School, was entering Willamette University.

July 12th we drove to the airport for the last time. Mary Jo was thirteen months old that day. Joe saw us off. He would finish his work and meet me in Los Angeles to drive east with me. (Secretly I suspected he would find an excuse to fly directly to Miami in coolness and comfort!)

Friends waved goodbye as the checkered flag went down. With Al Monsen at the controls we took off, over the empty house, over the lots we had planned to buy. Below was Harding Lake, then Big Delta, and soon the line of cut trees marking the Canadian border. Goodbye to Alaska's golden heart. Goodbye.

Mary Jo smiled and hummed in imitation of the motor's droning, her big, brown eyes wide with excitement. Margie Lou and Teddy buried their faces in paper sacks.

Margie Lou planned to keep a diary and write a book about the trip which she had titled "Mushing to Miami." One entry about this flight read, "We saw Lake LeBarge where Robert Service cremated Sam McGee in a poem."

At Whitehorse for a brief landing where a dapper Mountie checked our citizenship. Then south over Whitehorse Rapids, Lake Bennett, the White Pass and Yukon railroad tracks, and Skagway at the head of Lynn Canal. Glaciers in white sheets on the mountains. Down at Juneau on a green field with a new administration building, the blue ice of Mendenhall Glacier in the background. A night at the Baranoff Hotel and next day we boarded our steamer where Violet greeted us. She had gone by bus to Valdez and boarded there.

Purple and gold sunset fell as we wound through Wrangell Narrows. Then darkness closed down, darkness we hadn't seen for over two months. We liked our summer nights bright, not star-filled blackness.

I took delivery of a new Plymouth in Seattle, purchased through the garage in Fairbanks so that I had Alaskan license plates. Suitcases filled the trunk. A collapsible car seat and canvas bed were purchased for Mary Jo, together with a miniature toilet seat, diaper bag and kettle for bottles.

First we drove up the coast to Lynden to visit Marion and Dick, then to the Peace Arch on the border so we could say we had driven from one end of the United States to the other.

In Oregon we stopped over to attend the wedding, in Salem, of my brother Gus. We visited the YMCA camp near Tillamook where Teddy joined his retinue of seventy-five adoring small boys. Uncle Gus was about the finest man going, in Teddy's opinion. At the church in Salem he stood straight and handsome in a dress suit, watching his lovely bride come down the aisle. I was mortally proud of him as I thought back over the sixteen years since Mother died and left seven motherless children. The filled church was a tribute to the man he had become. A solid section was reserved for scrubbed little boys from the Y. Another Y boy played the organ.

The thermometer was 110° in Medford, and stayed high as we descended into the Sacramento Valley. We planned to spend several days with my brother Frank in Sacramento—where he was flying for the State Forest Service—but heat drove us quickly toward San Francisco and the welcome Bay fog.

Always anxious to dispense education and culture to my children, we 'did' San Francisco, the Golden Gate Park and the Natural history museum, lunch at the Cliff house, the afternoon at amusement concessions along the beach, dinner in Chinatown. Next evening, in a quiet motel in Monterey I asked what had impressed them most on that eventful day—the new bridges, the aquarium, Chinatown, what?

"I think," Teddy answered after due reflection, "that it was the little red car I drove around a track at the beach."

"I liked the waiter in Chinatown," Margie said. "He brought us tea and didn't even ask if we were old enough to drink it."

So much for cultural experiences!

Down to Los Angeles, hitting evening traffic on Wilshire Boulevard, fearsome after Alaska. Dad and Mother Barrows were living in an apartment. That night I struggled to open a window which seemed stuck at the top. Finally I unfastened some sort of arrangement so I could push it down. A few minutes later Mother came in and reproachfully closed it.

"You took off the burglar lock," she explained. "We only open it so many inches, then the lock catches and no one can climb in."

Our houses in Fairbanks didn't even have a key. I remember one night Joe got up to investigate a noise in the kitchen and found an inebriated prospector standing by the range warming himself before stumbling on toward his outlying cabin.

A wire from Juneau arrived. "On my way out stop will meet you in Los Angeles stop drive carefully stop Joe."

Grandpa Noyes, now ninety years old, was frail and feeble. He had a boarding place in San Jacinto right on the Main Street where he could visit with everyone who came up town. Children called him Grandpa, and most adults called him "Uncle Frank." As usual he couldn't understand why I kept moving from such outlandish places as Alaska and Florida. Why couldn't I settle down. How I wished I *could*!

"How can Mary ever find her way to Florida?" he worried.

"Some day," I still kept promising. "I'll have a home and there will be a room for you."

He shook his head. "I'm afraid it will be too late."

Joe wired from Seattle saying he must go to New York and then abroad on confidential survey work which would take at least two months. I could go on to Florida, or wait in Los Angeles. How natural this upset seemed! But we were thrilled for his opportunity. Four days later he wired that he would sail that morning on the Norwegian steamship "Savengefjiord" for Norway, Sweden and Iceland to do some survey flying with Bernt Balchen for Pan-Am.

Dad's and Mother's apartment was small and we couldn't stay there indefinitely. Violet wanted to find work. Schools would open soon. I decided to go on to Florida anyway, rent a house and get located.

Joe's brother, Bob, flew in on a business trip from Chicago where he was an executive for United Air lines, in charge of their reservation department. I hadn't seen Bob in years. He looked older, thinner, handsomer, but so tired! Dear Bob, who died at age twenty-seven, with a promising future ahead. Died leaving a wife and a four-year-old son, and a place which would be forever empty in our hearts.

As I loaded the car to start our transcontinental journey a final wire came from Joe. "Trip indefinitely postponed. Leaving immediately for Miami. Meet you there." And we had thought he was on the ocean.

Our drive was long and hot, across the southern part of the United States in August in a car without air conditioning. It was 117° in Needles at nine in the morning. We detoured to visit the Grand Canyon and took side trips through Navajo land to see the Petrified Forest, the Painted Desert.

139

"It's nice not to have a man along," Vi commented. "They're always in such a hurry to get from here to there, they never stop to look at anything along the way."

A Mexican restaurant in Albuquerque, the Indian pueblos of Santo Domingo, San Felipe and San Ildefonso. Adobe houses, beehive ovens, children herding goats, lovely black glazed pottery. Santa Fe where we wandered through the museum in the old Palace of the Governors, a building old before the Pilgrim Fathers landed.

The Texas Centennial Fair at Fort Worth where the livestock pavilion was the only cool spot. Gradually the dryness of west Texas changed to sticky humidity. At Marshall, Texas it was still 95° at ten o'clock at night. We went to sleep with an electric fan swirling overhead but I woke, perspiring, in the night to find it silent. Next morning I asked who had shut it off.

"I did," Teddy admitted. "I wanted to save the hotel's electricity."

Into Louisiana with lush greenery everywhere. Cotton pickers in the fields. Dirty service station restrooms with signs "White Only." Flea-bitten mules hauling rickety carts with wobbling wheels, carrying cotton to the gins. Unpainted shacks with stone chimneys at one end. Unpainted little towns where people sat on the porches, fanning languidly. A dirty ferry boat across the Mississippi.

Our principal remembrance of this trip is heat. New Orleans offered delicious food, but our tour of the city lost its glamour and romance under the glaring sun. The old quarters seemed merely decaying and dirty, with smells of sewage and dead fish. I told Violet authors and artists came here in search of atmosphere.

"It may be atmosphere to them," Vi retorted, "but it's just a bad smell to me."

We purchased pralines, bananas and a mammy doll, then headed across Mississippi where Spanish moss hung on the trees. Red hills, pine woods, thermometer at 110°. The baby was red, restless, drooping pathetically. Across the Suwanee River and we were in Florida. At dark there was a terrific thunderstorm, lightning flashes lighting up the orange groves. The children cowered in terror, never before experiencing such a storm.

The Florida lake region where snowy white birds rose from the water, flying over the orange groves. Ah, this was better! Perhaps Florida wasn't so bad after all. We drove along the Atlantic coast, passing boom towns with exotic architecture in cheap stucco which peeled and cracked. Scrub palmetto covered subdivisions. After eleven days of driving and sightseeing from Los Angeles, we arrived in Miami.

August is not tourist season. The weather was hot. Almost every afternoon we had rain squalls. Lightning and thunder frightened Mary Jo and she woke screaming from her afternoon naps under a mosquito net. When the rain stopped the sun came out, the ground steamed, and the air was sultry and humid.

Joe had rented a house near Dinner Key, the Pan American base. Every day he went there in his blue serge uniform, white shirt and necktie, carrying a heavy brief case full of textbooks. The pilots studied hard to pass examinations for a Master Captain rating. Navigation, blind flying, international law, Spanish, and heaven knows what all. We all practiced semaphore signalling. We learned the ship's flags which are run up in the harbor. We talked first aid. Dinner Key was a college for captains, those taking post-graduate work for a Ph.D. in aviation. They learned their navigation by flying across the Caribbean, preparing for those longer projected flights across the Pacific and eventually the Atlantic.

Our house was banked with shrubbery which made ideal hiding places for insect and reptile life and cut off any vagrant breeze which might blow in. The dining room walls were decorated with huge mounted fish with glassy eyes which made us feel like cannibals whenever we ate a fish dinner under their malevolent stares. There were no bookcases. The kitchen's cupboards were high and it lacked any streamlined efficiency.

In Fairbanks I ran a seven room house, did the washing and ironing, cooked for five or six people and baked my own bread. I coudln't understand pilot's wives who had one or two servants—that is, until I tried to do the washing by hand at the kitchen sink. There was no washing machine, not even a laundry tub. I soon discovered that, at the very least, I wasn't acclimated. Perspiration gushed from every pore even though I stripped to shorts and halter. Finally I gave up and sent the washing out. It was done in Coconut Grove, in black kettles boiling over open fires in the backyard. The soap must have been pure lye because the sheets fell apart as if they had melted.

Teddy was self-conscious in his new white shorts. "I wonder what the gang in Fairbanks would say if they saw me in this sissy rig?" he muttered.

The road to Dinner Key was lined with palms and flowering hibiscus. At the coast guard station amphibians rode at anchor. We turned into the wide driveway at the terminal and proudly parked in the area reserved for pilot's cars. The terminal was exciting, with a blue and silver color scheme, with airplane history stenciled on the walls, and with a huge illuminated globe revolving in the center of the room. How could it help being exciting? It

141

might sell tickets, check baggage, inspect passports, but to what exciting places, such romantic regions.

"Plane loading for Havana, Cienfuegos, San Juan, Trinidad and points in South America."

Joe checked out on each run, beginning as copilot on a little amphibian called "The Duck" which flew to Merida and Belize. When he became captain in charge and took out the huge clippers to Nassau and Havana we nearly burst with pride. We stood on the balcony at five o'clock to watch the clippers come in.

"That's *my daddy* landing!" Teddy informed all and sundry in his proudest, loudest tones. "That's my daddy who is captain of that clipper."

The beaching crew waited by the dock. The gangplank was out. The crew came ashore, the captain leading, all the men trim and neat in uniforms and white caps. The whole operation was like a fairy tale, an Arabian Nights story of flying carpets. "And I want to roll to Rio—roll down to Rio—and I want to roll to Rio some day before I'm old—" Kipling's song ran through my mind. Now one could roll down to Rio, seated comfortably in a sound-proofed compartment of a big ship of the air. It was only a day or two from Miami to South American cities.

Names conjured images of the old Spanish Main. Port-au-Prince and voodoo drums, Christophe and his citadel at Cap-Hatien. San Juan, with memories of Ponce de Leon, where bells ring in the tower of the oldest church in the New World. Pirates, penal colonies, spices—yes, these were modern magic carpets.

When the clipper docked we hurried downstairs to wait while the pilot checked in, wrote up flight reports, exchanged comments about the trip and gossiped a bit. When Joe emerged he handed Teddy his brief case, swung Mary Jo into the air so that she crowed with delight, and headed for the car. Teddy staggered under the weight of the brief case. "Gee, Dad, this must have a ton of bricks in it."

"Oh, those are just my meteorology and navigation books. And a Spanish grammar and a book of international law and another on first aid."

At the other end of his flight he often had several hours to study. And in the evenings he went to the terminal for meteorology lessons.

"There's Betelgeuse," he pointed into the star-filled sky. "See, that brightest star in the constellation of Orion. And that's Acturus, one of the brightest stars visible to us."

On days he didn't fly he took blind flying practice in the "Link Trainer" at the airport, performing maneuvers under cover, watching the instrument board. All these captains were veteran pilots. Many were ex-Navy men or, like Joe, they had barnstormed from aviation's early days. Some had been with Pan-Am since the beginning of overseas runs. Ed Musick began down on Key West in flights across to Havana. They had thousands of air hours to their credit.

At home Joe quickly shed his heavy uniform. His white shirt was wet enough to wring out, literally without a dry thread. Why couldn't the crew dress in cool linens, or why weren't the clipper cabins air-conditioned?

Violet prepared to apply for a job at some Pan-Am station in a romantic, faraway port. But after her third restless night on a hot bed, in a breathlessly sultry room, she announced that she was going back to Oregon.

"You have to stay," she said, "but I don't. I'd rather go back to Alaska. There's no sense in living in a place where I'd be hot and miserable all the time."

We arrived on Sunday. Thursday morning we took her to the train (air-cooled) and wished in our homesick hearts that we were heading for the Northwest, too.

Our house had bugs. Huge, hairy spiders dropped from the ceilings. I killed an ugly scorpion as it came from behind the couch, its wicked tail lashing as it headed toward Mary Jo's bare ankles. There were cockroaches in the kitchen, huge flying beetles as long as your little finger. Ants, large and small, red and black, flying and walking. Weevils in the flour. Silver fish eating the glue from the backs of our books. Lizards ran up the screens eating flies. Mary Jo's crib had a net to protect her from mosquitoes. Mosquitoes are a pest in Alaska, too, I'll admit, at least for a few weeks in the summer, but we had never needed bed nets.

A kind neighbor took the children to a Sunday School picnic on the beach. They came home with itching feet and it developed that they had hookworms. Cat-and-dog hookworm, creeping larva—there were different names for this parasite. The doctor froze the feet with ethyl chloride. Margie, sobbing with pain, said, "I wouldn't mind having my feet frozen if I could be ice skating back home."

For weeks I bandaged their poor sore feet which were covered with nauseating blisters and little red tracks where the worms burrowed under the skin. It was Christmas before Margie could wear any shoes but open sandals.

"These things don't bother in the winter season when it's cooler," I was told. "Only during the rainy time when they breed in the sand."

A newspaper reporter saw our car's Alaskan license and came to interview us. She encountered Teddy first as she entered the yard.

"Aren't you thrilled to be in this heavenly country after the frozen Northland?" she asked.

"Naw!" he answered emphatically. "I want to go back to Alaska."

"But I can't put that in an interview!" she protested.

Finally she wrote up the interview from Teddy's viewpoint with a headline: "PAGE THE CHAMBER OF COMMERCE. TEDDY DOESN'T LIKE FLORIDA."

Alaskan periodicals played this up with great glee, but it didn't increase our popularity in Miami.

However, every place has some compensations. We saw beautiful sunsets over the feathery palms. We went fishing down on the Keys. We made friends with other Pan Am personnel. We ate wonderful grapefruit, a huge hamper full for one dollar. We had avocado trees in our own yard.

I've always been afraid of snakes, from childhood days on the Colorado prairie where we watched for rattlers. On trips into the Everglades we saw cotton-mouth mocassin snakes on the highway. Skins of diamondback rattlesnakes were on sale and we were warned about deadly little coral snakes. A baby alligator, about eighteen inches long, perhaps a fugitive from the Everglades, moved into a pond in our back yard. His tiny teeth looked razor sharp and Mary Jo wouldn't venture into the yard. Neither would I after dark in case his mamma had come looking for him. We shook our slippers every morning in case a scorpion was hiding in them.

Joe was happy because he was busy, doing interesting work he loved. He had no more management worries, just the joy of flying the big clippers, of becoming every day more proficient in blind flying and navigation. He was trying to cram a two-year course into one year, with only a high school education in contrast to many pilots who were college graduates or had Navy training. Passage of his Master Captain's exams would bring our desired transfer to the Pacific division.

In contrast to his busy days time hung heavy on my hands. I had a maid to do the housework so I enrolled in classes at the ramshackle building then housing the University of Miami. And during the season a friend and I operated a gift shop in the Miami-Biltmore Hotel, selling imports from along the Clipper air lines. We didn't even make good wages, but we didn't go broke and we did have fun.

My sister Edith came down all the way from Oregon by bus. She said she had saved $140 and was afraid someone would want to marry her for her money, so she decided to travel. Joe was now flying longer trips, through to the Panama Canal, and I was glad of her company.

Margie Lou finished the sixth grade and was active in Girl Scouts. Teddy was a Cub Scout and went to a summer day camp where he learned to swim, dive and paddle a kayak. Mary Jo was now two and talked with a southern accent learned from the maid.

Again we were in a hot summer rainy season with thunderstorms every afternoon and sticky, humid air. Once hurricane warnings were posted, but the storm passed over harmlessly.

The family in San Jacinto who had boarded my grandfather were selling their business and moving to another town. They were unable to find anyone to undertake his care as he was getting very feeble. He was also lonesome for someone of his own family. My mother had been his only child so we grandchildren were all he had.

California schools would begin early in September. Joe was slated for a vacation in October and assured that he would be transferred to the Pacific by November, probably in October so he could vacation there. We decided that I must go to California to rent a house and get settled before school started, and he would be there within six weeks. Edith would go with me to help me drive. In the meantime, Joe would move into a small apartment and concentrate on his Master's exams. Teddy reminded him that he often said their noise bothered him when he was concentrating on some difficult problem.

The morning of August 15th, almost a year after we arrived in Miami, we loaded the car. Sleep had been almost impossible in the sticky heat, even with an electric fan buzzing all night. When I stripped the beds I saw that our pillowcases were wet with perspiration. Our necks were covered with prickly heat and Mary Jo was broken out with heat rash.

Joe bought me a new car to drive west. He would either sell the Plymouth or drive it out when he was ready to leave. We picked a box of avocados to give to relatives along the way. If only Joe were going with us—

As we turned onto the highway Mary Jo began to sing a song her sister had taught her, "Golden Gate, we're coming to you—"

CHAPTER SIXTEEN

Captain of the China Clipper

Our route took us along the edge of the Atlantic. We breakfasted at Fort Lauderdale under the baleful eye of an immense stuffed fish. My taste didn't run to stuffed fish, carved coconut heads or painted flowers on turtle's shells. I don't like still life pictures of dead birds with bloody breasts over my dining room buffet either.

Around Lake Okochoobee were the first hills we had seen in a year. Through orange and grapefruit groves to the Bok Singing Tower but there was no concert as this was not tourist season. At Saint Augustine we went sightseeing to visit the oldest house in the United States, the oldest schoolhouse, the Fountain of Youth where we drank the water to restore lost childhood. Margie Lou wondered what it would do to two-year-old Mary Jo. We saw the point where Ponce de Leon had landed and pictured the conquistadores in their heavy armor. Teddy loved the old fort, especially the dark dungeons, and was entranced with all the skeletons in the Indian communal burying ground. I shivered at the grizzly sight of eighty or more skeletons stiffly laid out with bony toes pointing to the east and ghostly hands crossed over bare rib cages.

Back roads took us into Georgia and that night in a motel we pulled up blankets and rejoiced in feeling cool again. Green rolling hills of South Carolina with here and there a white-columned house. The Great Smoky Mountains with hills which began to look homelike. We wound down into a glorious sunset at Knoxville.

As I registered at the motel I tried to chat with the woman proprietor.

"Isn't it a beautiful drive up into the mountains?"

"I dunno. I hain't never been up thar," she answered. "When I gits up into the mountings my haid swims, so I hain't goin' up thar."

Teddy wished for buckskin clothes and a long Kentucky rifle as we followed Daniel Boone's trail through the Cumberland Gap into old Kaintuck. A rickety ferry took us across the Cumberland River and Margie could hardly be restrained from inquiring about feuds of the gaunt mountaineers we saw. We had ice cream cones at a town with the fascinating name of Marrowbone. One town had a courthouse square in the center. The road was porly marked so I drove around the courthouse and continued on. About a mile out of town I decided to check our route.

"Is this the way to Glasgow?" I asked of two men leaning against a fence.

One came over, draped himself against the car and thrust his head in the window to say, "You better go on up to Columbia. They can tell you thar."

Road maps indicated that Columbia was thirty miles out of our way so we turned back. All day we took back roads, enjoying the mountain scenery, and about four o'clock arrived at the Mammoth Caves.

Entrance fees were $2 apiece, $8 for four of us, with Mary Jo going free. We dug sweaters out of the car, though skeptical of needing them. But inside the cave the air was delightfully cool. We enjoyed seeing the stalactites and stalagmites though I grew tired carrying a heavy child up and down ladders. Mary Jo whimpered at the underground world and cried when we climbed into a boat on a little lake. She preferred daylight.

One sunny morning we stopped at The Old Kentucky Home at Bardstown, a majestic house set with velvety lawns, containing great square rooms filled with old furniture. We wanted to move in, until we saw the kitchen.

"We can tell that the woman who lived here didn't do her own cooking!" Edith exclaimed at the sight of a huge fireplace, long-handled pans and a trough for scalding newly butchered hogs. No running water in the house, only bowls and pitchers on the old-fashioned commodes. I'll take modern plumbing.

Kentucky blue grass. Beautiful horses. Whiskey distilleries. Across into the fertile farmlands of Indiana. Margie and I tried to select a home fitting the description of Gene Stratton Porter's home in "Laddie", my favorite childhood book and now hers. We learned that the author's home had been farther north. Across the Wabash River into Illinois. There were no vacant rooms in Salem, everything was full. The hotel lobby swarmed with shouting, gesticulating men.

"No vacancies," said the clerk. "We're having an oil boom."

Finally we stayed at a tourist guest house. This was Abraham Lincoln's town but Edith and I thought of that other Salem and sent postcards to Gus and Dottie, out in Salem, Oregon.

In Jacksonville we visited the big, gracious home of our cousin, Vera, who had children of Margie's and Teddy's age. The children were taken to Springfield to the state fair and we visited Lincoln's tomb and his Springfield home. We ate fried chicken, corn on the cob, cream so thick one dipped it with a spoon. Many relatives lived in the area and the children behaved themselves in unprecedented fashion. Teddy was so quiet when we visited two elderly cousins that I thought he must be ill.

"You're not much like your father," one of them told him. "He was always so lively, never still a minute. Why, the last time I saw him, your grandfather was spanking him out on that very lawn."

A day's drive into Iowa brought us to Aunt Stella's home, a huge ancestral house occupying a whole city block in Eldora, and filled wall to wall with heirlooms. After dinner we drove to a quiet little farm at Steamboat Rock where my dear Aunt Edith and Uncle Frank now lived, strangely transplanted from the banks of Oregon's Chetco River—and as homesick as I had been in Florida.

Margie and I were fascinated with relics of family history. We saw the ox yoke my great-grandfather had used when he drove from New York to this farm and homesteaded it. "This land has always belonged to the Moore family," we were told. Uncle Frank had inherited it from an aunt. That night when I tucked Margie Lou into a wooden bed which had belonged to her great-aunt's grandparents she sighed happily, "The ancestral bed."

West between fields of corn waving high over our heads. Across the muddy Missouri into Nebraska where corn grew drier and more stunted until finally only bare stalks were left and swarms of grasshoppers smashed against our windshield.

This was the Oregon Trail! Markers showed the progress of westbound wagons, covered wagons pulled by plodding oxen. I visioned patient, weary women trying to cook beside the trail, washing clothes in the little streams, caring for small children, even giving birth to babies along the way. Men went west for adventure, to explore and settle new lands. Women went because they must follow their men, pulling up their roots, leaving homes and families, enduring hardships and dangers.

Ghosts of Pawnee Indians, Ogallallas, Arapahoes also stalked the trail.

At Ogallala, Nebraska we left the Lincoln Highway and headed south over the rolling sandhills to Fleming, Colorado. The little town looked much as it did when we left it in 1918. Fourteen miles south across the prairies, past dried up wheatfields and gaunt windmills, we came to New Haven where a union school replaced the one-room building where I went through the grades. The buildings on our old homestead were deserted and lonely on the treeless plain. The great barn which had been my father's pride was sagging into ruin; house windows were broken. I told Edith I sat under that same windmill holding our brother Gus when Dad came out of the house to tell us we had a little sister. I showed the children the cellar door under which I once found a rattlesnake. Memories were thick of our hard-worked mother who died so young, our scattered family, old playmates who had moved away or gone to a land where there are no droughts or dust storms.

My first school teacher, Ruth Hall, planned a party for us in her new homestead house. In the midst of the party the room filled with choking dust and we ran to close windows. Dust was everywhere, on dishes, on beds, in ridges on the floor. In those dust bowl years the prairie was cruel to its adopted children.

From Fleming we went west toward the Rockies and north into Wyoming. The road climbed toward the Continental Divide. Fort Bridger again evoked pictures of tired men and ox teams, of covered wagons with canvas now ragged and dirty. The road forked and we left the Oregon Trail to turn into Utah which the Saints had made to blossom as the rose, and at sundown drove into Salt Lake City.

We toured Temple Square. Mary Jo discovered the acoustics of the tabernacle before the guide could drop a pin and I had to take her out so others could listen to the lectures. The guide asked those who wanted to hear about polygamy to raise their hands. Teddy's shot up, but afterward he said he didn't quite understand what it was:

When we planned our trip back in Miami Margie's wish had been to see the Mammoth Caves and Teddy's to swim in Salt Lake. I parked at a bathing beach and stayed in the car with Mary Jo while Margie, Edith and Teddy swam.

"You really can't sink, Mom. Even *you* could swim in that water," they said.

Salt flats and desert and long stretches between towns, then over the Sierras and down into the Sacramento Valley. At the state line we had to unload every bit of baggage while officers searched our car with a fine tooth comb. The Florida license must have provoked them and they didn't want me to smuggle in a fruit fly. We were there nearly three hours.

"Has California seceded from the Union?" I asked as cars were held up, license plates ripped off as bewildered people had to buy new tags before they could enter the state. These were still depression years and poverty-stricken folks were leaving the dust bowl states, Steinbeck's "Grapes of Wrath" people.

At last the Carquinez bridge, the oil tanks of the North Bay, and into Berkeley where we could see golden lights strung along the two big bridges.

"Mary Jo, there's the Golden Gate bridge."

She shook her head in disbelief. After twenty days on the road she had given up reaching the destination about which she sang.

Next day I found a nice house high in the Berkeley hills, a house with a beamed ceiling in the living room and a stone fireplace.

There were Navajo rugs on the floor and bookcases crammed with early Pacific Coast histories. From the windows we had a breathtaking view of the University campus, the bay and the spans of the bridges, with the lights of San Francisco in the distance. After I convinced the University professor who owned the house that Mary Jo didn't eat books, we rented the house and moved in.

As soon as we unpacked I drove to southern California and brought Grandpa and his few possessions home with me. He had a suitcase full of clothes, a book of faded dageurrotypes, some recent photos of his family, a cherrywood clock with wooden works and a New Testament in large print. He settled into the front bedroom downstairs where he could move his rocker out onto the terrace on sunny days. He and Mary Jo immediately became great friends. While he sat reading his Bible she rode his cane around the room, stopping to look up into his face and smile.

"Don't us kids have fun, Grandpa?"

Margie Lou and Teddy went to school. Young cousins found their way up the hill on Sunday evenings, and I loved having them.

Joe's October vacation was cancelled as the tourist season was heavy and he couldn't be transferred yet. Every letter contained the same old uncertainties. We hoped for him at Thanksgiving and planned on him for Christmas when all the clan gathered—Dad and Mother Barrows, Marjorie and Jean from Los Angeles, my brother Frank and his family from Sacramento. But he was still in Florida.

In January the Samoan Clipper went down in the South Seas, carrying with it Ed Musick and the rest of his gallant crew. I went to the memorial services in San Francisco's City Hall and saw Cleo Musick in black. Near was Marian MacLean, widow of the navigator, sitting bravely with an arm around each of her little girls. The wives and the children who are left behind—I've known so many of them.

Grandfather fell one evening as he was crossing the living room. His fragile old bones snapped and his hip fractured. Two weeks later he was gone. He was 92, a grand old man, stern and rugged perhaps like the granite of his Vermont hills, but with Vermont strength of character.

At last Joe arrived from Miami. Almost at once he was scheduled out on a check flight across the Pacific to Honolulu, Wake, Midway, Guam, Manila and at last to Hong Kong. We all went to the Alameda terminal to see the giant clipper taxi out into the Bay and take off over the Golden Gate bridge on its long six day journey to Asia. Teddy boasted to all of his friends.

"After all, there aren't many kids in the United States who have a dad who is captain of the China Clipper!" he bragged.

One Sunday while he was gone on the three week's trip we drove across the Berkeley hills and in a new subdivision at Orinda we found a house that would be ideal for us. It sat upon an oak-covered hill with an acre of ground. The front windows framed a sweeping view of the valley. The walls were of adobe, with deep-set windows. There was a beamed ceiling, a stone fireplace, plank floor, a big sun-filled patio. The kitchen was tiled in yellow and white. One of the several bedrooms was paneled in knotty pine. The basement had a recreation room, also finished in knotty pine.

"Mother, this is paradise. This is our Shangri-la!" Margie cried. She had just seen the movie, "Lost Horizon."

I walked through again, mentally furnishing the rooms in Monterey style furniture with Mexican and Indian rugs. Here the children could grow up and bring their friends. This was a house for gracious living. Did I dare dream of a home at last?

Edith went downtown one early morning to shop. On her return she hurried to the radio and, white-faced, began twisting the dials to get a news report.

"I just heard the end of a broadcast on the car radio," she said. "Something about a clipper missing—"

A clipper— missing—

Somewhere over the wide expanse of ocean Joe was flying a Clipper. He and his crew and passengers were winging their way east above the water. Or were they? It seemed ages before Edith got another news cast. The Hawaiian Clipper was missing somewhere near Guam, believed down with all aboard. But Joe had been flying the Philippine Clipper. He should be east of Guam, approaching Hawaii. Soon we heard again, "Captain Leo Terletsky was in command of the missing Hawaiian Clipper. A Japanese boat has reported seeing an oil slick on the water. No trace of the missing flying boat has been found."

Joe had met that crew on Midway Island, where they all spent the night on those blobs of sand formerly inhabited mostly by comic gooney birds.

We went soberly to the terminal to watch him come in, flying a giant mechanism which had last touched at the Hawaiian Islands. Twenty-four hours it had been aloft, its crew steering it through the night, its motors throbbing steadily.

As it approached I remembered the first time I had seen Joe, fourteen years before, as he stunted over San Jacinto in a crazy Jenny and brought it down for a dead stick landing in a cow pasture across from Grandpa's house. A foolish kid, people called him then, wasting his time on a hobby which would never be of practical use.

I recalled the succession of planes in which we had flown. The Hisso-Jenny which landed us on the hills on our honeymoon. The cabin plane in which we barnstormed up and down the Oregon coast. The old Fairchild 51 we flew across the continent, and which Bob Reeves was now landing on Alaskan glaciers. The Bellanca that carried the mail down the Yukon River that severe winter. Each a little better, a little more powerful than the last. The huge Ford freighter (the 'tin goose') which Joe and Al Monsen flew from New York to Fairbanks over the Great Bear and Great Slave Lakes. The Fleetsters. The twin-motored Lockheed Electras in which he dedicated the Fairbanks-Juneau mail run. Then the Commodores and Sikorskies in Miami, flown to Nassau and Havana and on down to Baranquilla and Panama.

Now he was Captain on the China Clipper line. Now he had the finest position open in aviation. And his story was the whole history of commercial aviation, from the red-haired boy barnstorming in a rickety Jenny to the uniformed captain on the world's greatest air line.

The bulletin board read, "Transpacific Crossing Number 228. Captain Barrows."

Proudly we watched the big silver bird settle gently on the water. Proudly we watched the crew climb out and march ashore along the ramp, Captain Joe in the lead.

"Hi, daddy," Mary Jo shouted, waving her arm. He smiled but did not relax his dignity.

"That's my daddy. That's *my* daddy," she announced loudly.

Into the terminal to report in, and then out to the car, now swinging Mary Jo up in his arms.

"We've found a wonderful house," I told him. "Just what we've always wanted. Some of the other pilots are buying homes. Can't we be settled at last? When you've rested let's go and look at it."

Joe shook his head. Was the gesture that of an eagle's wary motion when it fears a cage, fears clipped wings which might bind it to earth?

"Buy a house? Be settled?" he answered. "I don't want that. I never want to be settled. I want to go on from here to fly the Atlantic."

The Atlantic! Then farewell to our Berkeley hills. Goodbye to my dreams of security and a permanent home.

"I don't want to buy property," Joe repeated. "I don't want to be tied down. I want to be free."

The End

EPILOGUE

We were divorced in September, 1938, and Joe immediately married a girl he had met in Miami.

The children and I went up to Puget Sound where I enrolled in Western Washington College of Education at Bellingham. Here I earned a degree and a teachers' certificate.

The first thing I did was to buy a house, an old two-story house on Lake Whatcom. The lot had seventy-five feet of lake frontage and a dock for our rowboat. I used as a down payment the last bond Grandpa left me, after I paid for his funeral expenses. Our home became a favorite gathering place for Margie Lou's and Ted's friends, for swimming parties, wienie roasts on the beach, and for dancing on the big front porch.

At last we had a permanent home and security—but without Joe.

Pacific Alaska Airways pilot, first time in uniform.

House on 10th and Cushman which burned while we were en route to Skagway, spring of 1935. Note round ventilator holes

Joe and his youngest daughter, Mary Jo. 1936

New name, new affiliation—Pacific Alaska Airways, subsidiary of Pan American

Twin engine Lockheed which inaugurated the Fairbanks-Juneau mail run, April 2, 1935

*Pan american Airways maintenance superintendent
and pilot, Fairbanks. Skis designed by Joe*

Teddy at Dinner Key, Miami, in front of one of the flying boats

Flying boats on the Miami runs

"Page the Chamber of Commerce—Teddy Doesn't Like Florida". Miami, 1936

Clipper taking off at Honolulu on Trans-Pacific Flight Number 228. Captain W. J. Barrows in command. 1938

Home on Lake Whatcom, at Bellingham, Washington. Bought in September, 1938